Fiber-Wire Beads and Jewelry

Lisa Vann

Published by

Krause Publications
700 E. State St.
Iola, WI 54990-0001

Please call or write for our free catalog of publications. Our toll-free number to place an order or obtain a free catalog is 800-258-0929 or please use our regular business telephone 715-445-2214.

Step-by-step photos by Mark Goros.
Project designs by Lisa Vann, unless otherwise noted.

Library of Congress Catalog Number: 2002105084
ISBN: 0-87349-445-8

Acknowledgments

I'd like to extend my sincerest thanks and gratitude, first of all, to the artists who have participated in this book. Their significant talents, effort, and enthusiasm for the challenge provided me with a constant stream of fresh, energizing inspiration.

Lydia Borin is a designer, author, instructor, storyteller, and beadwork historian. She is the owner of www.beadcrochet.com and www.beadwrangler.com, exciting bead and fiber information Web sites.

Fiber artist, Linda Hendrickson, is passionate about tablet weaving, ply-split braiding, tribal designs, unexplored possibilities, and the meditative qualities of handwork. She has written numerous articles and books, and she is an enthusiastic and patient teacher well known to students in North America and England.

Susan J. Lewis specialized in Enameling at Kent State University and has exhibited her work in many galleries and museums. She teaches Jewelry Fabrication and Precious Metal Clay classes at the Boca Raton Museum of Art in Boca Raton, Fla., where she is the head of the Jewelry department.

Susan Berkowitz has been a polymer clay artist for about 10 years. She incorporates beadwork, wire, and fiber into her polymer clay jewelry and vessels. She is a vice-president of the San Diego Polymer Clay Guild.

Mishi Campbell is an experienced bead and jewelry designer, influenced from an early age by her father, a well-known metalsmith and gemologist.

Suzanne Pineau is a knitter and teacher and has been the owner of Knitting of La Jolla for three years. She has been in the knitting industry for 25 years and previously owned the Needlework Attic in Bethesda, Md. Suzanne began knitting at age six and was teaching it by age 14.

I'd also like to thank a number of behind the scenes folks: Amy Tincher-Durik for her assistance in convincing me to write this book; Jodi Rintelman, my editor, for her ever-ready support and timely efforts.

Appreciation is extended to Sherri Callosso for her right-on-the-money assistance in bead choices.

A very special note of thanks goes to Mark Goros, my photographer, for his excellent eye, unswerving support, and monumental patience.

Finally, my thanks to Jesse and Mia for their constant enthusiasm, interest, and help. I couldn't have done it without you all.

Table of Contents

It took time for the concept of *Fiber-Wire Beads and Jewelry* to mature. I originally began concentrating on fiber after writing my first book, *Make Wire Beads*. Having worked primarily with thin-gauge wires, twisting fibers with them flowed naturally from that body of work. For many years previous, I'd attempted to combine fiber and wire with, at best, frustrating results. The successful integration of the two materials eluded me.

To suddenly realize that success was the result of something as simple as twisting the fiber between two thin-gauge wires was humbling. How could something so very simple have escaped me for so long? I was consoled by reminding myself that artistic revelations often occur only when the time is right, and finally it was. Holding in my hand a now-pliable strand of twisted fine silver and hand-dyed silk, my mind leapt into visions of artistic possibility that I knew would continue to evolve far into the future.

I dubbed my new, colorful, soft, but durable strand a "wiber." It would be any fiber-and-wire-combined strand that maintained its stability and could be used as an independent artistic element. It could be used to build many things, just like plain wire. Only the wibers had the added dimensions of color and texture.

Making beads was an easy application for wibers. Simple twisted wibers produced delicate metal patterns when wound on a dowel to make a basic bead. Winding the twisted wibers on other, thicker wire reminded me of basket weaving. What else could I do with a wiber? What other kinds of wibers could I make?

Techniques and jewelry design applications formed along with a number of preconceived ideas about this new fiber-wire work. Some of the initial assumptions I had were very accurate. As I continued to explore my new medium, I discovered many were just plain wrong.

I originally assumed any fiber-wire work I created would take on a strong ethnic appearance and style. Not so. What I learned instead was that fiber-wire beads and jewelry are versatile; the style of any piece of jewelry can run the gamut from classic to contemporary. The designer determines the style, not the wiber.

I also assumed that fiber-wire beads would be secondary beads, unable to carry a piece or focal presence by themselves. Untrue. While the bead construction methods are simple, they can be embellished for intricacy and are well capable of holding the focal point of a piece of jewelry.

Another assumption I made was that for a fiber-wire jewelry piece to be successful, a good amount of metal would need to be incorporated into the design. But it isn't necessary to include metal. Beads can easily provide sufficient reflective quality to add visual depth. Fiber jewelry can also stand alone simply by virtue of the strength of its color and textural attributes. Adding metal to fiber, however, brings not only metal's structural attributes but its significant decorative ones as well. The synergy between the two elements had explosive potential.

Fiber-wire was teaching me a great deal about itself.

As the concepts for this book shifted, changed, and grew, so did my goals. What originally started as a simple bead application turned into a prolonged exploration into the artistic boundaries of a wiber. How far could I take this little strand? Just how versatile was a wiber? What were its limitations and problems? I decided to take the challenge.

In doing so, it was essential to stretch beyond fiber-wire beads in jewelry. In its simplest form, a wiber could be used to bind other elements together or to form a bead. In a larger sense, it had potential as a primary construction element. The wibers, so much like tiny cords with body, surely could be woven or used in macramé, braiding, or basket weaving. I wanted to tackle the application of wibers to other textural, woven crafts like crocheting. I wanted to offer up some of that successful exploration to the readers. We decided then to add a chapter on crocheting with wire.

While pleased with the way that chapter and its projects were developing, there was something unsettling. A dimension was missing. It finally occurred to me that in looking at the projects, readers would have little awareness of the process that occurred in developing the pieces. They would be completely unaware of the many, tiny design decisions that inevitably occur during the evolution of a piece.

All that excellent learning was missing when I looked at the carefully detailed project instructions … as if it all evolved that seamlessly. Each piece of jewelry, every project, had a unique design process and story. If I'd learned so much during the development, wouldn't readers as well? I just had to include some of those stories.

That thought ultimately led me to also invite six artists from totally different disciplines to participate in this book. While I originally starting hunting for fiber jewelry artists, somehow that didn't have the right feel. I wasn't looking for anything that had been done. I was looking for what hadn't been done and the artists to help create it.

I chose an enamellist, a weaver, a bead crochet and bead artist, a polymer clay artist, and a knitter. I approached them all, uncertain but excited about the potential outcome and adventure. We all worked differently. In some cases, we chose to collaborate and in others, the artists listened, asked questions, and then went off to work their own unique artistic magic. As a result, two of the artists have contributed projects to the latter, more challenging part of this book. The others either contributed to the gallery or in collaborative efforts.

Their willingness to step into the experiment has added a rich and intriguing dimension to this book. I'm both proud and grateful to include their works here.

Chapter 1

What You'll Need

There's clearly no substitute for using quality tools and supplies in jewelry making. Likewise, there's no substitute for having a good working knowledge of the range of available supplies and where to locate them. The more information you have, the easier it will be to choose the ones that will work best for your own particular needs.

It actually takes very few tools and supplies to make even the most complex fiber-wire bead or piece of jewelry. Here's a short list of what you'll need to start:

Small wire cutters
Chain-nose pliers
Needle-nose pliers
A few different-sized round dowels from ⅛" to ¼"
Fiber, yarn, or thread
Embroidery floss
Ruler
Scissors
Fabric glue and/or a glue stick
Dritz Fray Check™
FiberGard™ fabric sealant
Clear acrylic spray sealer

Investing in a set of high quality hand tools will be money well spent. It makes good sense to spend some time shopping and researching these tools. Even the simplest tools have a variety of characteristics to consider. You'll want to make sure your tools suit you, your own hand, and your working style. Individual comfort and quality are equally important requirements.

EURO TOOL™ offers an extensive line of quality tools. If you're new to wire work, I recommend you start with the Value Series line of pliers. On the other hand, if you're committed to working with wires and metals and you're looking for some slightly higher end precision tools, the Relentless line is well worth your consideration. EURO TOOL hand tools are available from authorized distributors nationwide.

The three most important tools you'll need are: a good flush wire cutter, small needle-nose pliers, and a pair of chain-nose pliers.

Wire cutters are a necessity, and there's a wide variety to choose from. Flush cutters are preferred since they leave one side of the cut wire flat and easy to sand to a smooth finish. This helps reduce the amount of time spent filing and sanding wire ends. The other section of the cut wire will have an angled cut to it and require more filing to finish.

Needle-nose pliers are an essential tool for doing wirework. The body of these pliers is cone shaped, tapering to thin rounded ends. It's those tiny ends that allow access to hard to reach areas, almost like an extension of your own fingers. Needle-nose pliers are also used for making wire loops and rounding wire, and they're extremely good for curling up the ends of thin-gauge wires. The tip of the round-nose pliers is used most frequently for forming and shaping the ends and fine areas of beads and jewelry.

Chain-nose pliers are an excellent companion to needle-nose pliers. Similar in their tapered ends, chain-nose pliers are different from needle-nose pliers in that they're flat on the inside. Small square tips allow for a firmer grip on wire than do needle-nose pliers. I use these pliers frequently to compress wires and other small parts. They also come in handy for making a square bend in a wire or to open and close small loops.

Precision flush sidecutters (wire cutters).

Needle-nose pliers.

Chain-nose pliers.

What You'll Need

Dowels, either solid or hollow rods, come in a variety of different materials and shapes. In this book, they're mainly used as a forming tool to assist in shaping wire and for building fiber-wire beads.

Round dowels are the most common, easily found, and extensively utilized in this book. Other dowel shapes include: square, octagon, half round, triangular, and oval. While more difficult to locate, these dowel shapes produce some interesting effects when wire is wound around them. However, if you're lucky enough to come across some of these dowels, you'll need to make sure any edges are sanded down smoothly so the wire slides off easily. Putting cornstarch on the dowel first can also help the wire slide off more easily.

Dowels are available in a variety of materials and lengths. You can easily find wood, brass, and aluminum dowels in hardware, art and craft, art supply, and hobby model stores. Plastic dowels often come in unusual sizes and shapes but are more difficult to locate and can be much harder to work with.

Since dowels are used essentially as forming tools, the most important things to consider are how easily the wire or metal will slide off of them and how durable they are. Round, hollow, metal dowels are the best choice.

Since brass and aluminum dowels are the most commonly found metal dowels, if you have a choice, pick brass. Brass is a dense, heavy metal, whereas aluminum is very soft, lightweight, and too easily bent. While aluminum dowels can work well as a tool for forming beads, their innate softness makes their lifespan short.

Brass dowels come either hollow or solid and, for most applications, I prefer the hollow ones. Large, hollow, brass dowels are strong enough to resist even the tightest winding. By and large, these dowels hold up well.

I recommend using hollow as opposed to solid brass dowels with this caveat: hollow dowels come in a variety of wall thicknesses. The thinner the wall, the greater the chance of bending the dowel. If you tend to pull your wire very tightly, hollow dowels can bend. Choose a hollow dowel that has at least a medium wall thickness. Hollow brass dowels are lightweight, sturdy, and generally easy to work with.

While this may seem like a minor point, something as simple as choosing a hollow over a solid metal dowel can make quite a difference in your working comfort. Particularly if you're using dowels a lot in your work, the extra weight of a solid brass dowel can eventually cause discomfort. Those little babies get heavy!

If you live in a remote area and/or find it hard to locate dowels, it's fairly easy to find substitutes. Metal crochet hooks and knitting needles work well. Rummaging through kitchen drawers may also produce some good dowel substitutes.

Since the majority of fiber-wire beads are built on round dowels, you'll want to invest in several, ranging in size from ⅛" to ¼".

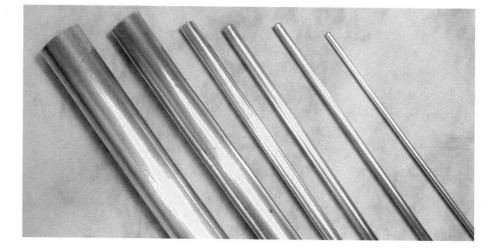

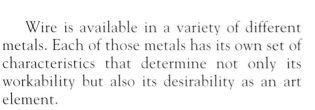

Wire is available in a variety of different metals. Each of those metals has its own set of characteristics that determine not only its workability but also its desirability as an art element.

Different types of wires have different attributes regarding composition, hardness, and pliability. Of the metal wires, fine silver, sterling, brass, and copper are used most frequently in this book. Understanding their individual characteristics will help you choose your own preferred wires.

Metal wires can come in their pure form or as a compound of metals known as an alloy. Alloys are generally made either to increase the workability of a wire or to produce a particular color of metal.

Hardness of Wire

Wires come in three degrees of hardness—hard, half hard, and dead soft—for use in different jewelry applications. Ear wires, for example, are generally made with half-hard wire. Dead-soft wire can be easily reworked.

Metal Wires

Pure silver, also known as fine silver, has the highest silver content. It's the whitest-colored silver as well as the softest. While most wire gets harder the more it's worked, fine sil-

ver does not harden as quickly or as much. Although it's generally too soft for many other jewelry applications, fine silver wire can be used effectively for a number of wire jewelry projects. While it's difficult to find very thin-gauge sterling silver wires, they are easily available in fine silver.

Sterling silver is an alloy of copper and fine silver, if the ratio is 925 parts fine silver to 75 parts copper. This proportion gives the resultant sterling wire greater strength without altering its coloration too greatly. Sterling silver is often the preferred metal for jewelry making because of its combined appeal in terms of price, durability, malleability, and decorative appearance.

Copper is an almost pure metal, malleable yet sturdy, and in ready supply. With its rich color and flexibility, copper is a desirable metal for jewelry and has roots in ancient history. While often used for prototyping metal jewelry, copper holds some promise for more extensive use in jewelry today.

Brass, an alloy of copper and zinc, is a hard metal. Its color ranges from bright yellow to greenish or reddish yellow, making this an appealing metal for jewelry making. Yellow brass has the greatest amount of zinc in it and is the most malleable of the brass alloys. An inexpensive metal, brass has wide applications for jewelry.

Colored Wires

Colored wires are a wonderful addition to fiber-wire work. Their ability to enhance, coordinate, and contrast with the rich colors of fibers makes them an exciting and valuable design asset. Another advantage that makes colored wires a particularly appealing option is the fact that they don't tarnish.

Colored aluminum wire, known as anodized aluminum, is available in a number of vibrant colors. Very soft, pliable, and easy to use, it also can be sensitive to scratching and is more costly.

Niobium wire is also vibrantly colored but quite stiff, and it can be difficult to manipulate. Its strength and vibrancy however, do make it appropriate for certain jewelry applications.

Non-tarnishing silver and brass wires from Artistic Wire® are recent additions to the wire worker's options. They have strong appeal for fiber-wire work, as does Artistic Wire's broad color range of copper-coated colored wires.

Sizes of Wire

Wire is sold in varying thicknesses, commonly known as the gauge of the wire. The most important thing to remember about gauge size is that the higher the number, the thinner the wire. For example, a 14 gauge wire is fairly thick compared to a 24 gauge wire. The majority of the wires used in this book are thin-gauge, ranging from 20 to 26 gauge.

The gauge and type of wire you choose has everything to do with the degree of success you'll have in creating your fiber-wire beads and jewelry. By following some of the bead recipes in this book, you should rapidly acquire a solid, working feel for your own preferred types of wire. You'll also gain a working knowledge of a variety of wires, without losing a lot of wire through trial and error.

In designing your own fiber-wire creations, you'll want to decide whether you want the wire to be primarily functional, decorative, or both. Do you want the wire to complement or contrast with the fiber? How much do you want the wire to show? Are you using the wire primarily to hold down the fiber? How do you want the wire to relate to the overall color palette and structure of your piece?

The most important thing to consider when choosing the wire type for your fiber-wire beads is pliability. That is, how well does the wire hold its shape and stay in place? All wires have different degrees of pliability and strength and will perform differently, depending on how you bend them and how they interact with individual fibers. A good rule of thumb is to test wires before using them.

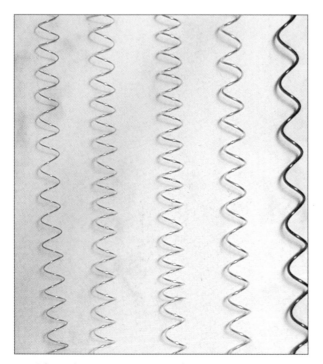

From left to right: 28, 26, 24, 22, and 20 gauge wires.

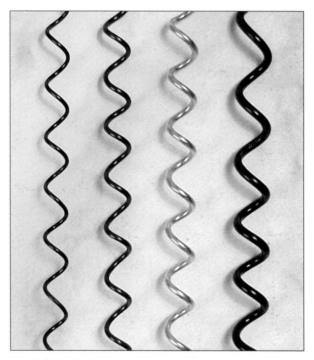

From left to right: 18, 16, 14, and 12 gauge wires.

Candy stores have often been used to evoke yummy, salivating kinds of imagery. With the near dizzying array of fiber products today, the same type of imagery comes to mind. With all of the new hybrid and synthetic fibers available, it's beyond this book to provide a truly comprehensive list.

That said, it does help to have at least a preliminary grasp of the kinds of yarns available. Technically speaking, yarns and threads are composed of animal, plant, and synthetic fibers. These fibers are also frequently combined with one another to produce an astounding array of hybrid yarns.

Yarns are manufactured in a wide variety of ways. There are: nub yarns, boucle, chained and knitted yarns, component and brushed yarns, combined, chenille, eyelash, and woven yarns, all with their own methods of construction and individual manufacturing processes.

With the enormous variety of fiber products available, making choices can become a bit overwhelming. In addition to having its own set of characteristics, each type of fiber performs differently when combined with wire. Here's a partial list of fibers that I've used successfully in making fiber-wire beads (in order of working difficulty from easiest to hardest):

Cotton

I started making fiber-wire beads with small skeins of cotton embroidery floss. It was inexpensive and easy to acquire a large variety of colors. Combining colors to create custom color palettes was a big plus as well. Cotton threads lay very nicely on top of one another, and the surfaces tend to stay in place. Mercerized cotton is a shiny, stable fiber that also works well and adds the option of added reflectivity.

Wool

Just as there many different kinds of sheep, there are many different kinds of wool. Wool has some elasticity to it and tends to easily retain its shape when combined with wire. Wool threads and fibers can be coarser and, from that perspective, they are a bit rougher to work with. This coarseness, however, does add to wool's easy workability—it lies quite nicely on itself. Another consideration with using wool in fiber-wire jewelry is the way it will feel against the skin. Some wool blends may be softer and provide a better solution.

Silk

Silk fiber by itself is a bit hard to work with. Silk blended with wool or cotton, however, works very well. These blends tend to be a bit more slippery than cotton. When winding silk fibers, a little extra effort is needed to get the threads to go where you want them. It's worth the effort though. Silk-wire beads are utterly gorgeous. The sheen on some of these yarns adds a dimension of considerable beauty when married with metal wire.

Rayon (viscose)

Made from processed wood pulp, rayon tends to be strong. It's also stretchy and can be slippery, making it harder to work with and control. Rayon fibers also tend to unwind rapidly if tension is released during winding. Try them after you've had some success working with cotton, wool, or silk blends first.

While it's helpful to understand the working characteristics of fibers and yarns, the bottom line consideration is simply what works and what doesn't. These are the questions I need answered before I purchase a new yarn: Is the yarn slippery? How well does it react when compressed between thumb and forefinger? Does it look delicate or as if it might shred?

Will the texture of the yarn work well if twisted between wires? How will it perform with different gauges of wire? How durable is the yarn's construction? Finally, and of considerable importance, how will it feel against the skin?

Even if I get the wrong answers to some of those initial questions, when fibers and yarns are married with wire, some of what appeared to be questionable characteristics are still workable. For example, slippery fibers are frustrating to work with and I don't recommend you start out with them. However, I have worked successfully with slippery fibers. It can be done.

I advise you to start out with cotton and the other fibers listed above. After you gain a little experience, start testing other fibers and keep a log of your experiments. Finally, as you're starting out, I'd avoid the fluffier combination fibers and yarns. They're trickier, can be harder to work with, and the outcome can be unpredictable.

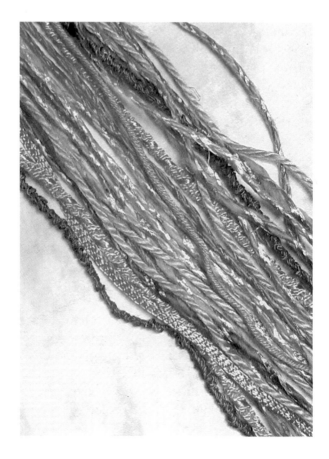

Jewelry Findings

Findings are small metal parts used to assemble jewelry. It's a good idea to pay attention to findings as you develop your jewelry piece. They may be named "findings" because they're often hard to find.

End caps, as they sound, are small parts used to cap off the ends of a jewelry piece. They are available in a variety of different shapes and materials.

A **bail** is a small, generally circular structure, primarily used to hang a pendant.

Jump rings are small wire circles used to connect other jewelry parts and, as such, have multiple applications.

Clasps are used to clasp finished jewelry pieces together, typically bracelets and necklaces. Clasps are as functional as they are decorative. As you're working, it's helpful to start envisioning the clasp that will work best with your piece.

Earring findings come in a wide variety of choices but are usually one of two kinds: post or hook. The post type keeps the top of the earring closer to the ear while the hook allows the earring to hang.

Head pins are straight, metal pins in varying lengths with small flat areas or loops on the bottom. Called the "head," this area functions to keep beads, etc. from falling off the bottom of the wire. Head pins are used for building earrings and for assembling and stacking other decorative items like beads.

Ear nuts are the small parts used to keep post earrings on the ear.

End caps and clasps.

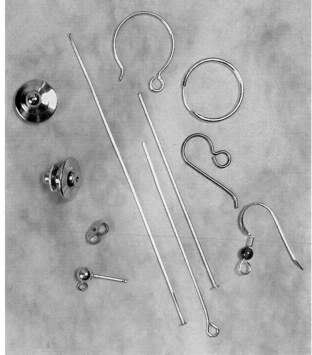

Head pins and earring findings.

Additional Supplies

Depending on the type of fiber-wire beads and jewelry you choose to make, some of the following additional supplies can be useful as well:

Needle files are slender metal files used to file off rough areas on end wires or metal. The Nylon Jaw Plier by EURO TOOL is a wire straightener that pays for itself very quickly by reclaiming otherwise lost wire. Simply pull the wire through the jaws to have it quickly straighten the wire.

Midas™ from Rio Grande is an anti-tarnish metal sealant.

Dawn™ liquid detergent is useful for removing grease and dirty residue from wires.

Dritz Fray Check is used to seal the ends of your wibers, and **FiberGard** spray by FiberGard Chemical Corp. protects your finished fiber-wire beads and jewelry.

E-6000™ is a brand of jewelry glue.

Metal polishing cloths are available from jewelry supply houses and are special cloths embedded with jewelry polish. They're easy to use and come in very handy when looking to clean and shine thicker-gauge wires.

Tarn-X™ liquid metal cleaner is very useful for cleaning thin-gauge wires.

White glue sticks can be helpful for making the glued fiber-wire beads, and **Sobo**™ craft and fabric glues are good for sealing the ends of the beads.

Finishing Products

Liquid metal antiquing solutions are available from jewelry supply houses. Depending on the brand you choose, this product will effectively darken wire anywhere from dark to light black. Steel wool is then brushed over the surface to allow some of the original wire color to show through.

Sandpaper in rough, medium, and fine grades can be used for smoothing the ends of heavier-gauge wires.

Steel wool is available in different grades and is used either to remove some of the residual antiquing solution (when used) or simply to rub on the metal to create a matte finish.

Chapter 2

Basic Techniques

Before you begin working with fiber-wire, there are a number of simple winding and finishing techniques that will help you on your way. The essentials for building, connecting, and protecting the projects in this book are provided in this chapter as well. Additionally, there are a number of terms, some unique to this book, that are necessary to understand.

Definition of Terms

Bead base: Refers to the layers of wire wound on a dowel. A bead base is used to support additional layers of wire and fiber.

Core wire: Can either be a short length of wire on which a bead is built or a longer, thicker-gauge wire used to build a larger piece of jewelry. Core wires, as supportive structures for beads, should be a heavier-gauge wire like 20, 18, or 16 gauge. For jewelry, core wires should be thicker yet, preferably of 14 or 12 gauge. The exception to this would be using two wires twisted together, like 16 or 18 gauge.

Fiber: Technically, yarns and threads are composed of fiber strands. For the purposes of this book however, the term fiber will refer to any yarn, thread, fabric, or fiber strand.

Gauge: Refers to the thickness of a wire. Gauge can be confusing because a larger gauge number indicates a thinner wire. Just remember that the higher the gauge number, the thinner the wire. A 32 gauge wire is almost hair-like, whereas a 14 gauge wire is like a small dowel.

Loop: Refers to each full circle of wire or fiber-wire made on a dowel.

Ply: Refers to the number of single strands of fiber in a yarn.

Strand: Refers to a single length of either fiber or wire.

Wiber: A wiber is a single strand composed of one or more fiber and wire strands joined together.

Work hardening: Occurs as you continue to manipulate metal. The more you work with a metal or wire, the harder it will become and the more difficult to move. If your wire becomes too hard, continued working may cause it to snap and break off.

How you wind your wibers, wire, and fiber will greatly affect the visual outcome of your beads and jewelry. There are some basic winding techniques that will help you make and control the look of your fiber-wire jewelry and beads. The beads as well as some of the jewelry pieces are essentially built by winding wire and fiber back and forth on dowels, other wires, or jewelry parts. Both the method and the care with which they are wound will ultimately determine the success of your fiber-wire works.

Two things determine the density or thickness of your fiber-wire pieces. How many times you wind the wire and/or fiber around the other elements is the first. The second factor is the thickness of the wires and fibers you combine.

Likewise, the shape of your bead or piece is determined by where you lay the wire or fiber as you wind. Finally, the wire winding technique you choose will determine the overall look of your fiber-wire piece. Three different methods of winding wire around dowels are used in this book.

The Straight Wind

The straight-wind method is used most often and simply involves controlling the wire a bit so that it's wound in a straight up and down fashion.

The Slant Wind

The slant wind involves purposefully slanting the angle of the wire to create a slanted-looking finished coil. The slant wind method is used most frequently to build the interior layers of a bead or to wind on top of a straight wound coil for a decorative effect.

The Random Wind

The random wind requires a different kind of precision—random precision. Thin-gauge wire is randomly wound back and forth on a dowel, building up multiple layers without placing one loop too closely to the previous one. The basic structure of the beads is composed of many layers of overlapping loops. For a more controlled look, the top layers of the bead can be loosely slant wound, either in just one direction or in a crisscross pattern.

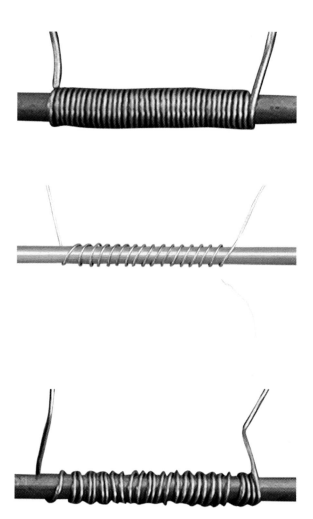

Building a Bead Base

To add stability, solidity, and strength to some of the fiber-wire beads, building a bead base is the first step.

1. Random wind one layer of wire on your dowel without cutting the wire.

2. Reverse direction and slant wind the wire the full length of your bead.

3. Repeat steps #1 and #2 to complete your bead base.

4. At the beginning of the fourth layer, add the wiber or fiber strand. Leave a few inches loose, and begin winding with both strands until the bead is complete.

Gradated Shapes

While there are a number of ways to create bead shapes, here's one that works very well, especially when attempting to gradate the shape of a bead or the ends of a bead. Placing progressively smaller dowels inside one another, telescoping them, allows you to gradually increase or decrease the size of the loops of a bead. The closer the size of the dowels to one another, the more refined the gradation will be.

Screwing Back the Ends of a Bead

Screwing back the ends of a bead will create a smaller, more rounded appearance on the ends. Simply take needle-nose pliers and gently twist the wiber clockwise. Likewise, should you choose to widen the ends of a bead, twist counterclockwise.

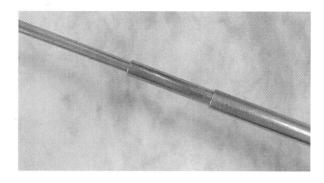

Making a Wiber

A wiber is a combined strand of wire and fiber. Most wibers are made by first cutting long, equal lengths of fiber and wire. In the majority of cases in this book, both strands are then folded in half together (making four strands) before they're twisted together. The wire strands, wound tightly, essentially bind and trap the fibers. Remember to always twist the strand in the same direction.

Ratio of Fiber to Wire

The successful creation of a wiber has to do with the specific relationship between the gauge of the wire and the thickness of the fiber. The wire, being the harder medium, has a tendency to cut into and compress the fiber. Depending on the nature of the fiber and its density and volume, the amount the wire cuts in will vary, creating different visual effects and patterns in the final wiber.

For example, if you use a thick or bulky yarn with a 28 gauge wire, the resulting wiber will have a delicate metal effect with more of the fiber evident. If, on the other hand, you use a thinner fiber with a thicker-gauge wire, more of the metal will show in your wiber.

Twisting Wire and Fiber

Twisting wire or wires and fibers together is fast and simple. There are basically two ways to do it. Both require one end to be secured in a vice. The other end is then twisted either with a hand drill and cup hook or with a pencil or dowel-like tool, depending on the thickness of the wire. You can either use a manual hand drill with a crank-like handle or a motorized one. I prefer the manual hand drill since I can easily control the speed of the twisting. Motorized hand drills can be very useful once you gain familiarity with speed adjustments.

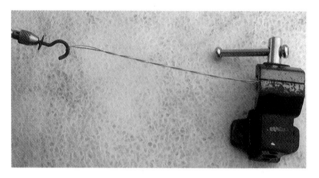

Sometimes it's easier to use a dowel or dowel-like instrument instead of either hand drill. This method comes in handy when you need to twist heavier-gauge wires.

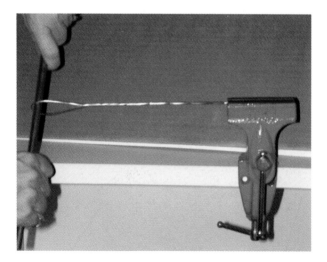

Tips for twisting wire and fiber

1. To ensure a consistent twist, both strands of fiber and wire should be of equal length and pulled taut together prior to twisting.

2. Twist at a slow to medium speed, periodically checking the consistency of the twist.

Stop here or just before.

3. As you continue twisting the strands together, you'll feel the joint strand pulling and getting shorter. When you feel a lot of resistance to the twisting, stop and remove the completed strand to prevent the wire from either twisting on top of itself or breaking.

Properly twisted wiber.

4. The minute the wiber begins to buckle, stop twisting. If you stop twisting as soon as you notice this occurring, the wiber can be easily smoothed out. Twist back slightly in the opposite direction, or remove the wiber from the vice and carefully smooth it out between your thumb and forefinger.

You've gone too far.

If you find that you've twisted too far, it's often possible to reclaim your wiber. But it's far easier to twist less in the first place.

5. Be aware that the twisting process will shorten the original lengths of wire and fiber strands one or more inches, depending on the particular wire and fiber used.

Cleaning Wire

If you'll be using silver, brass, or copper wires, you'll need to make sure the wire is clean to begin with. If the wire is tarnished, Tarn-X, a liquid tarnish cleaner, works well with thin-gauge wires. Depending on how dirty the wire is, you can also wipe or dip it in a solution of Dawn dishwashing liquid, which should effectively eliminate dirt and grease and restore some of the wire's sparkle.

Tarnishing of Metal

Metals tarnish or oxidize when exposed to the air, and unless tarnished metal is the look you're going for, the metal will need to be treated to prevent tarnishing before you combine it with fiber. Artistic Wire offers both silver- and brass-coated non-tarnish wires that provide an excellent solution to this problem. The finish alters some of the natural properties of the wire, however, it can be well worth it.

While there are a number of anti-tarnish products available, I've used Midas Tarnish Shield™ from Rio Grande to seal many of the wires in this book. It's a relatively fast procedure that involves soaking the wire in the solution for roughly 10 minutes. Follow the instructions on the label for additional information.

Another option for sealing your wires is to use a clear non-yellowing spray sealant, although it can be hard to reach all the sides of the wires. As a result, you'll probably need to give your wire a few light coats.

Colored wire is already tarnish proof, making it an excellent choice for fiber-wire jewelry.

Finally, always store your fiber-wire pieces in an airtight plastic bag to minimize tarnishing.

Protecting Wire

When metal tools meet metal wire, gouges, nicks, and scratches can be a frequent occurrence. As a result, you'll need to protect heavier-gauge wires by coating the tips of your pliers in one of the following ways:

Plastic tips for pliers are available, although I haven't tried these yet. In a similar fashion, you can dip the ends of your pliers into a liquid plastic solution. I tried this once, but found the added thickness on my needle-nose pliers to be a deterrent.

Although not necessarily the optimal solution, I wrap a thin layer of architectural tape around the tips of my pliers to prevent them from marring my metals. Architectural tape is white and very similar to masking tape. It's available in many art supply stores and has a top coating that's more durable than masking tape. It's also available in thin widths, which are perfect for wrapping the ends of pliers. Masking tape is a viable option if you have trouble finding the architectural tape, but it will need to be replaced often.

Now what if you forget to seal your wires before making your fiber-wire bead or jewelry? Since I've done this myself in my enthusiasm for working through an idea, here's a work around: Using a non-yellowing clear acrylic spray, give your finished piece two light coatings. This should help protect the wire from tarnish, although it can make the fibers in your piece feel a bit stiffer to the touch.

Protecting the Fiber

While the metal wire will tarnish if left out unsealed, it hasn't noticeably dirtied the fibers. Regardless of whether you choose to seal your wires, the fiber should be protected for longevity and durability.

You can choose to seal your fibers before or after you complete your fiber-wire project, although I recommend waiting until the project is completed in most cases. It's difficult to manipulate long strands without getting them caught or tied up in themselves. Finished jewelry, being compact, is far easier to move, allowing for thorough coverage and absorption of the sealant.

Simply spray your completed work (I've used FiberGard fabric sealant), and follow the drying instructions on the bottle. Since there is such a wide variety of fibers to choose from, I would strongly advise testing any questionable fiber prior to sealing an entire piece. You want to ensure that the colors of the fibers won't bleed or dilute when sprayed with a fiber sealant.

Finishing the Ends

Leave several inches of both strands of fiber and wire hanging loose before beginning to wind them on the dowel. Once you've wound both strands and created the first few layers of your bead, flip those strands back towards the bead and continue winding over them to integrate them into your bead.

Another way to deal with end wires is to tie them together at one end (the one you'll begin winding with). Make sure you wind over that knot in the first few layers of your bead.

Since it can be a bit difficult to secure a fiber when reaching the end of a bead, I suggest using a very small dab of transparent fabric glue.

Wiber ends

Securing the ends of fiber and wire strands is essential to using them as an effective art element. If you're using a twisted fiber and wire strand, wind one of the wires tightly around the rest to secure the bundle. After cutting off the excess, apply Dritz Fray Check to harden the fiber ends, prevent fraying, and help keep the bundle intact. When dry, add a small dab of a good fabric glue.

Crimp beads, although I haven't used them, may provide a secure as well as decorative solution for finishing fiber-wire strands.

Making Wire Loops and Hooks

Some of the projects in this book will require making small loops and hooks on the ends of wires. This is accomplished rather simply by using the jaws of needle- and chain-nose pliers.

Above. Use the base of the needle-nose pliers to form a partial loop or circle.

Left. Make a right angle bend in the wire with chain-nose pliers.

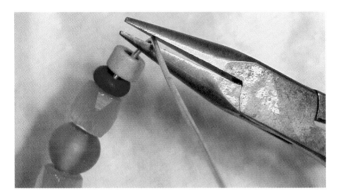

Filing and Sanding

Although thin-gauge wires are too delicate, the ends of heavier-gauge wires will need some filing and sanding. Needle files are used first to smooth down the rough ends of cut wires. Angle the file to point upward, and gently but firmly file up and around the entire outside of the wire. As you're doing this, allow the file to move up and on top of the wire.

Filing is intended to remove the biggest defects, and sanding gradually removes and smoothes out the smaller ones. Begin sanding with a rough-grade sandpaper. Then switch to a medium grade, and finish with a fine grade.

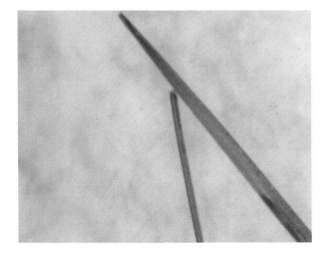

Basic Techniques

Adding End Caps and Clasps

Using wire to add end caps to a neckpiece is quite straightforward. Simply string the end cap over a thick wire extending from the end of the jewelry. To secure the cap, use a small dowel to wind one or two loops of wire once the cap is in place.

Adding clasps with wire is only slightly more involved. If the stringing wire is thin-gauge, it's wound one to three times either around the loop on your clasp or (if you're using jump rings as well) around the jump ring. If you've used a heavier-gauge stringing wire, simply open the jump ring using two pairs of pliers and close it using flat-nose pliers.

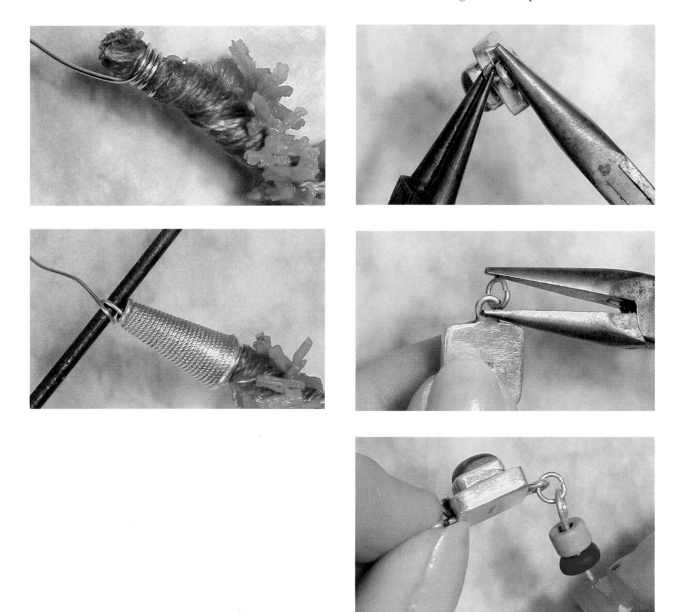

Antique Wire

Liquid, black antique products work well for darkening wire. Depending on the particular brand, you can either submerge the wire in the solution or brush it on. Buffing with a fine-grade steel wool allows you to remove excess.

Where to Begin

Being able to incorporate fiber with all its astounding color and texture is incredibly stimulating and inspiring. So where do you start?

Inspiration for any creative effort can come from a wide variety of elements. In the case of fiber-wire jewelry, the compelling spark can be color or the particular twist and composition of a fiber. Maybe there's a new technique you've been waiting to try out or a fabulous glass bead you've been hoarding.

No matter where the origin of your inspiration comes from, you'll benefit from having a system in place to manage your elements and your inspiration. Here's how I eventually managed mine:

After spending many months collecting my cache of unique and interesting fibers and beads, I started forgetting about certain prize pieces. I'd accumulated such a fabulous cornucopia of parts that I couldn't keep track of them all. I needed to organize.

While I'm sure many of you already know how to do this, working with such a multitude of diverse, colorful materials was fairly new to me. I started small piles of goodies based on different color palettes. As the "palette piles" grew so did my own enthusiasm. Each pile and color palette was more luscious than the last and no matter where my eye rested, inspiration abounded.

Now here's the interesting part: every time I walked past that amazing pile of piles, I got so excited that I'd actually become distracted from what I was doing. The colors were utterly glorious, each palette almost screaming, "Pick me, pick me." I'd inevitably find myself magnetized to the table.

I eventually started rerouting my path to avoid the piles just so I could get some work done. While usually not lacking for inspiration, this was an entirely new level of inspiration for me. I eventually resigned myself to the fact that I'd never get to use all the color palettes for this book, and that I'd simply have to choose the strongest ones. I did find considerable calming, quiet inspiration knowing that in creating the palette piles, I'd managed to contain the explosive synergy and distracting allure of all the elements. Pleased with this solution, I added a small notebook log to the end of the table to chronicle design ideas as they arose. Now I get to walk by my palette piles anytime I choose, confidant that I've not only managed the inspiration but captured it.

Take What You See

Experimenting with new art materials and techniques is tremendously exciting. Exploring and pushing the limitations of those materials can feed itself, often opening paths that never existed before or widening ones you're already on. There's nothing like this kind of adventure and it's all yours.

When I started mine, years ago, in my first art class, a professor began the semester with what I considered a shocking and provocative statement. He said, "Nothing is original. Look all around you and then take what you see and make it better." I didn't believe him then, and I certainly don't believe him now. But he did make me think. His words, jaded and limiting, were one of the best things anyone has ever given me. He challenged me to be original, to find some way around his cynicism. I've carried those words around with me for years, taking them out every once in awhile, just to test my own progress and mileage.

What I also learned from him was to find inspiration everywhere I looked. Determined to find that originality he didn't believe in, I examined art and design, looking for reassurance of the existence of true originality. Concerned and disappointed that he might be right, he taught me to begin to find my own originality. To do that, I knew I could start by looking at everything around me first and at least try to make it better.

While the project designs in this book are copyrighted and intended only for your personal use, you are encouraged to use them for inspiration in your other works. As you go through this book, hoping that you find some inspiration, take what you see and try to make it better. It's a good place to start and can lead you to an even better one—your own originality.

Chapter Three

Twisted Fiber-Wire Beads and Jewelry

Twisting fiber threads and wires together is one of the fastest and easiest methods of making a good, solid wiber. It's speedy, requires little in the way of equipment, and creates a wiber with a lot of design potential.

Twisted wibers have an especially appealing synergy between the wire and fiber. For the twisted wibers in this chapter, there is almost an equal ratio of fiber to wire, with the wire sparkling delicately from in between the fiber areas. We'll use these wibers to create beads as well as jewelry that incorporates fiber-wire beads with other materials. This chapter also applies these delicate wiber strands to existing jewelry.

Tips for Working with Twist-and-Wind Wibers

1. Make sure your wiber is twisted tightly before beginning a project. The tighter the twist, the more secure the wiber will be.

2. The most important thing to consider when making twist-and-wind wibers is the ratio of wire to fiber. There needs to be sufficient wire strength to trap the fibers securely between the wires and hold them in place.

3. The thinner the gauge of the wire used, the more pliable the bead will be. Whenever you use only a few thin-gauge wires in your wiber, the final bead will be softer and more flexible.

4. The symmetry of a twist will vary depending on the nature of the fiber used. The smoother the fiber, the greater the chance of an evenly-spaced wire pattern. If you use an irregular or nubby fiber, the wire will likely cut into the fiber irregularly.

5. As you wind or rewind your wiber, you may notice it starting to unwind a bit. It's then necessary to gently re-twist those areas between your thumb and forefinger.

6. Before beginning to work with your wiber, seal one end with a good fabric glue. When you cut off the excess from the other end of the wiber, you'll then need to seal that end as well.

7. If you're using metals that will tarnish, remember first to seal the wire with a clear spray acrylic or an anti-tarnish sealant before making your wiber. While I generally recommend using a fabric sealant like FiberGard on a finished piece, if you'll be manipulating the wiber a lot you may want to seal it first. To add additional protection to the ends of fiber-wire beads, apply Dritz Fray Check before final sealing.

8. Length estimates on wire and fiber strands for both the beads and the jewelry projects are generous to allow for both shortening in the twisting process as well as adjustment to fit personal jewelry sizes.

Twist-and-wind beads tend to be softer and more flexible since they're composed of thin-gauge wire and fibers. As a result, they are built on smaller dowels, so these delicate beads have small center holes for stability.

General Instructions:

It's very simple to make a twist-and-wind bead. Before you begin, however, it's essential to have a tightly twisted wiber in hand with one end already sealed with a good fabric glue like Sobo. Temporarily, on the other end, twist one of the wires several times around the entire end of the wiber. It will be sealed after you've built your bead to its desired size.

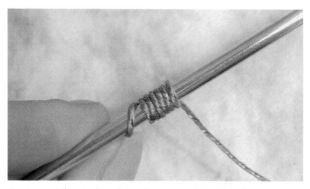

Begin straight winding the wiber around the dowel.

Continue winding the wiber.

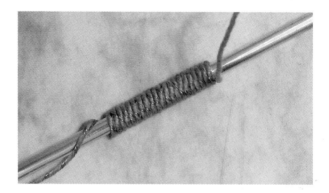

Wind the wiber until the coil is the desired length of the bead.

Bead #1:

Bead #1: Cut 3-foot lengths of both an aqua/pink viscose fiber (such as rayon) and 26 gauge copper wire. Fold them in half, and twist them together tightly. Secure the ends, and straight wind this wiber on a ¼" dowel. Tuck ends in to finish.

Bead #2:

Bead #2: Proceed as with bead #1, except use two 3-foot fiber lengths and only one wire strand.

This is a good example of the dramatically different looks that can be accomplished with one simple change. To continue enlarging a bead like this, try following this ratio: two fiber strands for each wire strand. Remember that the more wire strands you add, the harder the joint strands will be to twist together.

Bead #3:

Bead #3: Cut 3-foot lengths of multicolored blue/green fiber and 26 gauge copper. Fold the fiber and wire in half and twist them together tightly. Random wind that wiber back and forth within a ½" space on an ⅛" dowel. Finish the ends to complete.

When winding this bead, wind slightly more around the middle section of the bead.

For beads #3 and #4, wind a wiber on a small dowel, and then stretch it out.

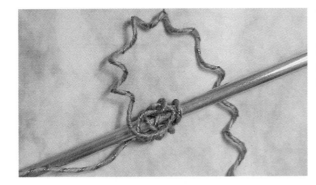

Random wind the stretched-out coil back and forth within a ½" area.

Use flat-nose pliers to compress and shape the bead.

Bead #4: Make a wiber as in bead #3, but use a black/gold fiber and a gold-colored wire. Straight wind that wiber around an ⅛" dowel, and then remove it from the dowel and stretch it out (this leaves symmetrical waves all along the length of the wiber strand). Random wind this wiber back and forth within a ½" space on an ⅛" dowel. Finish the ends to complete.

Bead #4:

Bead #5: Cut 3-foot lengths of a viscose-blend fiber and 22 gauge copper. (Using the heavier 22 gauge wire makes this a sturdy, solid bead.) Fold in half and twist together tightly. Straight wind this wiber around an ⅛" dowel. Next, slant wind the remaining wiber four times on top of that for the second layer.

Bead #5:

For beads #5, #6, and #7, slant wind the wiber over the original coil.

Bead #6: Cut 4-foot lengths of a viscose blend fiber and 28 gauge copper wire. Fold both strands in half and twist them tightly together. Using that wiber, straight wind a 1" coil on a ¼" dowel. Reverse direction and wind the remaining wiber loosely over the first coil. Wind each loop close together. Trim, secure, and tuck in the ends to finish.

Bead #6:

Bead #7: Begin by cutting a 1½" core wire of 18 gauge copper wire. Cut 30" of 28 gauge copper wire and a multicolored cotton thread. Fold both strands in half and twist together tightly. Begin winding the wiber tightly on the core wire, leaving about a ¼" at the end (this will become the end loop).

Wind the wiber along the core wire, stopping ¼" from the end. Reverse direction and wind the remaining wiber loosely around the first layer. Make loops on the ends to finish.

This is a smaller, more delicate version of the two previous beads.

Bead #7:

Black and Gold Dangle Pendant

This project demonstrates how simple it can be to add warmth and textural interest to a piece of jewelry. The centered fiber-wire loop provides a focal point for the pendant and contrasts nicely with the smooth glass beads above and below. This is a striking piece of jewelry that can be made in very little time.

- 1 small skein of black boucle
- 2 to 2½ feet of black satin cord
- 1 small spool of 26 gauge brass wire
- 14 gauge brass wire (or a large gold-colored circle)
- 1 large, black, ceramic or glass bead

- Additional glass beads as needed
- 3 brass head pins and jump rings
- Wire cutters, needle-nose pliers, flat-nose pliers, scissors, Sobo fabric glue, FiberGard

1. Depending on the size of the circle you make, you'll need at most a 2-foot wiber to cover it. Cut 50" lengths each of black boucle and 26 gauge brass wire. Twist them together tightly, and then spray on FiberGard to seal the wiber.

2. Wind the wiber tightly around the large gold-colored circle, and seal the ends with Sobo fabric glue. Make sure to leave a space between the beginning and end points of the wiber for the bead dangles.

3. Make a lark's head knot around the metal circle with the black satin cord, pull tight, and using three different head pins, assemble and attach all beads as shown. Make knots on the ends of the satin cord to finish.

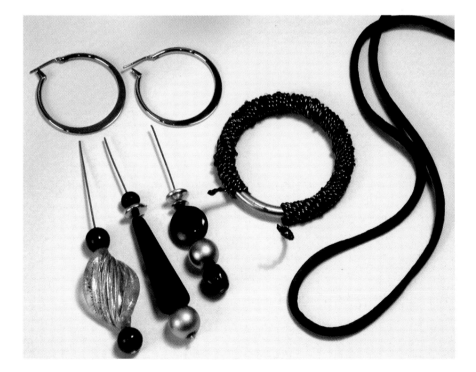

■ **Optional** ■

Make a matching pair of earrings with plain gold hoops like those shown.

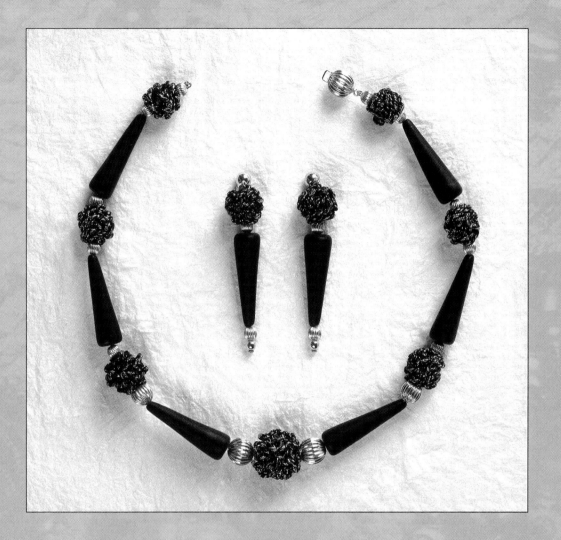

Like having the essential "little black dress" for your wardrobe, this necklace and earring set can become a staple in your accessories. The classic shape of the smooth, black vintage glass provided the inspiration for this piece.

Having finished all of the fiber-wire beads for this book, it was time to start incorporating them into jewelry. A trip to my favorite antique bead store quickly thrust me over the threshold between beads and jewelry. An appreciation for the beauty of those specialty beads immediately made me realize the possibilities for visual contrast by integrating glass and fiber beads. This ensemble is the result.

- Roughly 23 feet of a soft, metallic, black and gold fiber (for making the beads)
- 1 spool of 26 gauge brass wire
- ⅛" dowel
- 6 triangular, opaque, black, glass beads
- 18 small and medium textured, gold-filled beads

- Gold-filled necklace clasp
- Ball ear posts with loops
- 2 gold-filled head pins
- Needle-nose pliers, flat-nose pliers, wire cutters, scissors, Sobo fabric glue, FiberGard

To Make the Necklace:

1. Make seven Bead #4s (page 35). Make four just as the recipe says; make one twice the size; and make two slightly smaller than the original. Spray seal with FiberGard.

2. Cut a 2-foot length of 26 gauge brass wire (or beading wire). Begin stringing the beads on the wire in the sequence shown.

3. To attach the clasp, wind the 26 gauge wire neatly around both side connectors of the clasp.

To Make the Earrings:

1. Make two Bead #4s and assemble the beads as shown on the head pin. Spray the beads with FiberGard to finish.

2. Cut off the excess wire, leaving roughly ½" of the head pin extending out of the top of the earring. Make a small loop with needle-nose pliers, insert the end wire into the loop of the post and close gently.

Single Bead Neck Ring

This project is an enlarged version of Bead #5 (page 35). Minimal wire working skill, a few feet of brass wire, some fiber, and a bead allow you to create a simple but very contemporary eye-catching neckpiece.

If you aren't familiar with wire working, you could easily duplicate this neckpiece another way: simply purchase a standard neck ring, build the bead, and attach it with a head pin and bail. If you choose this method, remember that since head pins tend to be small, you'll need to make the bottom bead hole small enough that it won't slip off the head pin.

MATERIALS:

- 1 skein of four-ply wool fiber, multicolored red/purple/orange
- 2 feet of 12 gauge brass or gold-filled wire
- 1 spool of 24 gauge brass or gold-filled wire
- 6½" to 7" diameter pitcher
- Square gold bead (with hole large enough for 12 gauge wire to fit through)
- Wire cutters, flat-nose pliers, needle file, scissors, Sobo fabric glue, sandpaper

To Make the Neck Ring:

1. Cut an 18" length of 12 gauge brass wire. Form a circle around a vase or pitcher, measuring roughly 6½" to 7" in diameter.

2. Comfortably fit the neck ring to your own neck, and then use a flat-nose pliers to bend 3" of the wire at a right angle to the circle.

3. Again, adjust the neck ring to your own neck, leaving approximately 1" of wire to make a loop as the clasp. Trim the excess, and then file and sand the end of the wire. Firmly grasp the end with needle-nose pliers, and bend it into a wide loop. This is the clasp.

4. Fold together seven feet each of the wool fiber and the 24 gauge wire, and twist to form a wiber. Firmly wind one end of the wiber underneath the clasp and straight wind a coil on the 3" wire section. Leave roughly ¾" of plain wire near the end for the end bead. Wind the wiber back up the 3" length to create the second layer of the bead. When you reach the top of the bead, slant wind the wiber downwards towards the bottom of the bead.

5. Add the gold end bead. Make a "u" shape with the remaining wire end, and tuck it up into the bead. Finish the piece by spraying with FiberGard.

Twisted Fiber-Wire Beads and Jewelry

Sterling Cuff Bracelet

Winding a wiber around an existing piece of plain jewelry is the simplest thing you can do with a wiber. It can also produce some rather amazing and appealing results as evidenced by this bracelet.

MATERIALS:

- 6 feet hand-dyed viscose fiber, multicolored navy/magenta/green
- 6 feet 24 gauge sterling silver wire
- 1" width sterling silver cuff bracelet
- Metal-polishing cloth (to polish the cuff)
- Scissors, FiberGard, Sobo glue

Making the Cuff:

1. Fold 6-foot lengths of 24 gauge sterling silver wire and hand-dyed viscose fiber in half, and tightly twist them together to make a 3-foot wiber. You can vary the length of the wiber, depending on the size of your own bracelet.

2. Seal the ends, spray the completed wiber with FiberGard, and wind the wiber tightly around a sterling silver cuff bracelet. This one has 34 loops.

3. Tuck the ends in and under the back wibers to finish.

Twist-Wind-and-Coil Beads

If you'd like to make some more substantial fiber-wire beads, this is the technique for you. These beads are made by winding twist-and-wind wibers around another core wire for added heft, strength, and durability.

General Instructions:

1. Begin by making your twist-and-wind wiber. Next, cut a length of heavier-gauge wire to act as your "core wire."

2. Straight wind the twist-and-wind wiber tightly around the core wire, making sure to push all the loops tightly together as you wind.

3. You can choose one of two ways to finish the ends of these beads: Either continue winding to the end of the core wire and finish those ends, or stop 1" short of the end and use the remaining wire to make a finishing loop.

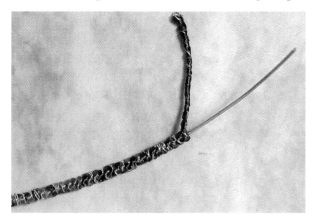

4. Wind this new wiber around a dowel and *voila!* The end result is a very hefty and interesting fiber-wire bead.

Tips for Making Twist-Wind-and-Coil Beads:

1. Read through all of the Tips for Working With Twist-and-Wind Wibers on page 32 before you begin.

2. Because of the double winding involved in making these beads, there is a strong tendency for the wire twists in the original wiber to start unwinding as the wiber is coiled onto the core wire. Just as with the twist-and-wind beads, you'll need to gently and periodically rewind or tighten those areas.

3. Before final sealing, protect your bead ends by applying Dritz Fray Check.

4. Remember to anti-tarnish wires before making wibers and seal finished projects with FiberGard for protection.

Bead #8:

Bead #8: Cut 4-foot lengths of a nubby fiber and 28 gauge brass wire. Fold both simultaneously and twist them together tightly. Next, cut a 6" strand of 20 gauge brass wire and straight wind the wiber on that wire. Finish the ends. Wind this completed wiber on a ³⁄₁₆" dowel to form the bead.

Bead #9:

Bead #9: Cut 3½-foot lengths of a viscose fiber and 24 gauge brass wire. Fold them in half and twist them together. Straight wind this wiber tightly around a 4" length of 20 gauge brass wire, and secure the ends. Next, cut a 4-foot length of 26 gauge brass wire, and straight wind this wire strand on the initial wiber, leaving space between the loops. Wind this new wiber on a ³⁄₁₆" dowel and tuck the ends to finish.

Notice the significant change in look by simply adding wire on top of the wiber.

Bead #10:

Bead #10: Cut 3½-foot lengths each of a very nubby fiber and 26 gauge copper wire. Fold them in half and twist them together. Secure the ends. Next, cut a 6" length of 22 gauge copper wire and straight wind the wiber onto it. Begin random winding 28 gauge copper in a haphazard way on top of the wiber.

Straight wind the entire wiber on a ¼" dowel (this is the size of the bead's center). To finish, screw back both ends of the bead (page 22) to create the shape as shown.

Straight winding wire at intervals on top of a wiber.

Compare the finished look of this bead with Bead #9. The look is hefty, relaxed, and very ethnic, as opposed to the more controlled look of Bead #9.

Bead #11: Cut 3-foot lengths of 28 gauge brass wire and a black/gold thread. Fold them in half together and twist. Next, cut 6" of 20 gauge wire, and straight wind the wiber onto it, leaving ½" of plain wire on each end to make the end loop. Straight wind this new wiber on a ¼" dowel, leaving ½" on each end. Spread out the loops and form into a spiral as shown. Finish by sanding the ends of the core wire and then winding them around a ¹⁄₁₆" dowel a few times to make the end loops.

Bead#12:

Bead #12: Cut 12-foot lengths of a blue/green fiber and 28 gauge sterling wire. Fold both in half and twist together tightly. Next, cut a 5" piece of 18 gauge sterling for the core wire. Straight wind the wiber onto the core wire, leaving ½" of plain wire on both ends to make the end loops. Place a ¼" dowel flush up against the straight wound piece. Continue winding the remaining wiber (without cutting it) around both the core wire and the dowel, leaving roughly ⅜" between loops. Gently press on the loops to gradate their size.

Bend the bead into a crescent shape. Make loops on the ends to finish.

You can also build this bead on a small dowel and then insert a core wire.

Bead#13:

Bead #13: Cut 12-foot lengths of a blue/aqua cotton fiber and 28 gauge sterling silver. Fold both together in half and twist tightly. Next, cut a 12" piece of 18 gauge sterling silver for the core wire. Straight wind the wiber on the core wire, leaving ¼" of the core wire on each ends. Secure the ends. Straight wind this new wiber on a ¼" dowel, and then gently screw back the ends (page 22) to form a ball.

Add end caps to finish.

Three-Bead Necklace

This necklace is a good example of how to use fiber-wire beads as a focal point. The curve of the croissant-shaped bead forms a graceful scallop around the neck. The opacity and sheen of the blue glass beads complement the intricate fiber-wire beads.

MATERIALS:

- 1 skein of 3-ply green/blue cotton fiber
- 12" to 14" of 18 gauge sterling silver wire
- 1 small spool of 26 gauge silver wire
- ¼" dowel (for building the beads)
- 6 silver beads
- 30 blue matte glass beads
- 4 green disc beads

- 14 navy spacer beads
- 8 lime spacer beads
- Sterling and lapis clasp
- Wire cutters, flat-nose pliers, needle-nose pliers, scissors, needle file, FiberGard, Sobo fabric glue, sandpaper

1. Cut a 12" to 14" length of 18 gauge sterling silver wire for the necklace. You will need to adjust this length to your own neck size.

2. Make three Bead #12s (page 45), add a silver bead on each end, and don't loop the bead end wires. Instead, leave ½" of core wire on each end. Make a right angle bend in that wire just above the silver bead.

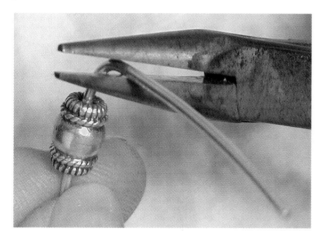

3. Make a small loop directly above the right angle in the wire on one of the fiber-wire beads. Slip the loop over the necklace wire and close the loop.

4. String the ten center beads as shown, and attach the other end of the center fiber-wire bead.

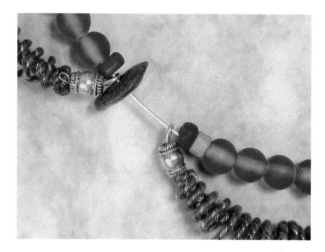

5. Continue assembling the remaining beads in the order shown. Using a needle-nose pliers, form loops on the end wires and attach them to the clasp. Spray the finished piece with FiberGard.

Twisted Fiber-Wire Beads and Jewelry

Spiral Earrings

These earrings are remarkably quick to make, using the same simple twist-wind-and-coil technique we've used for the beads.

MATERIALS:

- 6 feet of multicolored navy/magenta/green fiber
- 8" of 20 gauge sterling silver wire
- 6 feet of 24 gauge sterling silver wire

- Sterling silver ear nuts
- Wire cutters, needle-nose pliers, flat-nose pliers, needle file, FiberGard, Sobo fabric glue, sandpaper

1. Cut two 4-foot lengths each of 24 gauge wire and a multicolored fiber, fold in half together, and twist. Seal the ends.

2. Cut a 6" length of 20 gauge sterling silver wire and straight wind the wiber tightly around it, leaving about 1" of plain wire on one end to use as the earring post.

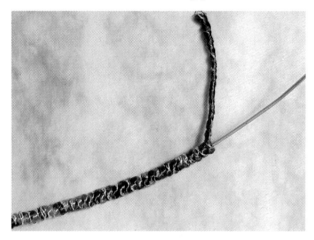

3. Using needle-nose pliers, make a small loop on the other end of the wiber and continue forming a spiral with flat-nose pliers. File and sand the first wire end, and gently curve it at a right angle.

4. Repeat for the second earring. Add a sturdy ear nut to the backs of the earrings and spray with FiberGard to finish.

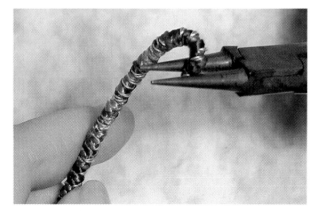

Twisted Fiber-Wire Beads and Jewelry

If you enjoy working in a more freeform fashion, then you'll find these next two neckpieces appealing. Having finished several of the jewelry pieces for this book, I decided to just have some fun and build whatever I wanted.

On a trip to Arizona several months earlier, I'd purchased several strands of mineral chips that had been patiently waiting for attention. I'd wondered how they would look strung on wire and twisted loosely with interesting fibers. Stabilizing them with some colorful wibers might work as well. This piece came together so smoothly and was so enjoyable it deserved to be included here.

- Several thin fibers in caramel, orange, olive, brown, rust
- 1 small spool each of 26, 24, and 16 gauge copper wire
- 1 small spool of 24 gauge Artistic Wire, brown, rust
- ¼" dowel
- Roughly 3 feet of mesh ribbon fiber

- Carnelion, ryonite, and butterscotch amber mineral chips
- End caps and clasp
- Wire cutters, needle-nose pliers, flat-nose pliers, needle file, pencil, FiberGard, Dritz Fray Check, E-6000 glue

/. Cut 2-foot lengths each of 24 gauge copper and a fiber. Knot the two together on one end, and then string four or five mineral chips on just the wire. Tie a knot with the two strands to lock the chips in place. Continue adding chips and knots along the entire strand.

2. Make four to five strands as above, altering the colors of the fibers and type of chips. Take each strand and loosely wind it around the first, moving chips as you wind.

3. Make two to three 3-foot wibers with olive and rust fibers and 24 and 26 gauge copper wire. Wind one wiber around after each grouping of two or three chip wibers.

4. Once all strands have been loosely twisted together, gently wind a thin, mesh ribbon fiber around the entire piece for added stability.

5. Wind rust-colored Artistic Wire onto a ¼" dowel for a few inches. Remove the coil from the dowel and stretch it out.

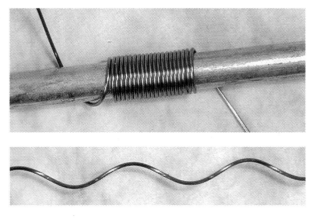

6. Loosely wind the stretched-out coil around the entire neckpiece, leaving at least 1" between loops. Then make two or three tight loops at each end.

7. Clip the excess wire off the ends and seal with Dritz Fray Check. Wind three loops of 16 gauge copper wire firmly around each end.

Slip end cap over this wire.

8. Wind 16 gauge copper around the end of a pencil to make the end caps. File and sand the end wires, and then put the cap through the wire extending from the end of the necklace.

10. Use a small dowel to make two loops above the end of the end cap and finish the ends. Attach the clasp to finish. Spray with FiberGard to finish.

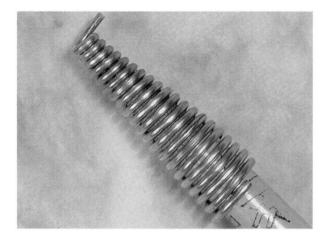

9. As a finishing touch, wind 26 gauge brass wire on a small dowel and then unwind it, stretch it out, and wind it loosely around the entire necklace. Tuck all wire and fiber ends up into the end cap.

One of the best things about building a bead collage with wire is that you can reposition the beads with ease and have them stay in place. Additionally, after building the piece, go back in with needle-nose pliers to tighten any wires. To tighten wires, simply grab them firmly with needle-nose pliers and twist clockwise. You also can bend the visible wibers into curved shapes to give a more flowing look to the piece.

Grapevine Neckpiece

This neckpiece is a variation on the Autumn Chips necklace, using beads instead of mineral chips. Another difference is that regular twist-and-wind wibers are used here to string the beads, so be sure a thin wiber can fit through the bead holes.

- At least 3 feet of two shades each of purple, olive green, and copper cotton embroidery floss and/or fibers
- 12" to 14" of 14 gauge copper wire (depending on your neck size)
- 1 spool of 26 gauge copper wire

- Various beads in a wide variety of sizes, shapes, and materials: purple, lavender, olive, fern, forest, and copper
- Wire cutters, needle-nose pliers, needle file, scissors, FiberGard, Dritz Fray Check, Sobo fabric glue, sandpapers

1. Cut a 12" to 14" length of 14 gauge copper wire, and form it into a circle (as with Single Bead Neck Ring, page 40). Fit the neck ring to your own neck and size, leaving 2" to 4" extra to make room for the beads.

2. Use the 26 gauge copper wire and your choice of fibers to make three to four wibers, 2 feet to 2½ feet long, and seal the ends.

3. String 10 beads on a wiber, and random wind it around the middle section of the neck ring, positioning the beads to face forward.

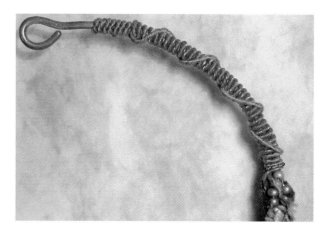

6. Make a simple hook-and-loop with the end wires. File and sand the ends.

7. Apply Dritz Fray Check to the ends of the fibers nearest the clasp. Let dry. Spray with FiberGard to finish.

4. Continue adding additional wiber and bead strands, compressing and working the beads into an interesting bead collage as shown. Wind the ends of the wibers onto the neck ring.

5. To finish, make two 2-foot lengths of purple and two 1½-foot lengths of olive-colored wibers. Wind the purple wibers tightly around the sides of the neck ring. Wind the olive wibers around and up the sides of the neck ring.

Chapter Four

Simple-Wound, Glued, and Trapped Beads and Jewelry

One of the main advantages to simple-wound beads is that no wiber needs to be made before you start your bead. This method simply involves winding the wire and fiber strands together on a dowel. Either of the strands may be dropped in the winding process to create alternate effects, and additional strands may be added at any point in the process.

Both strands are wound back and forth on the dowel, creating several layers. The fiber strand is wound underneath the wire strand in a random fashion so that the wire essentially holds the fiber.

The preferred fibers for making simple-wound beads are cotton, silk/cotton blends, and wool. Embroidery floss is excellent for this application since the tiny fibers tend to spread out during the winding process, causing the material to lay flat.

Simple-Wound Beads

General Instructions:

1. Begin building your bead by winding several layers of wire back and forth on the designated dowel to make a bead base. Random wind the first layer rather tightly, keeping the wire loops fairly close together.

2. Slant wind the second and third layers, creating a crisscross pattern. (For example: If your bead is going to be one inch long, slant wind from left to right for an inch and then reverse direction and slant wind back an inch.)

3. To add the fourth layer, leave about ½" of fiber loose in front of the bead end. Add the fiber strand to the wire strand. Begin winding with both the fiber and wire strands together.

4. Continue winding the fiber and wire (random wind, slant wind in one direction, then reverse) until you've created as many layers as desired.

5. The last few layers on fiber-wire beads will greatly affect the overall look of the bead, so a number of decorative options are possible. As you read through the individual bead instructions, those options will become clear.

Bead base pattern

Layer #1: Random wind with wire only
Layer #2: Slant wind with wire only
Layer #3: Slant wind with wire only, in the opposite direction
Layer #4: Add the fiber strand, and random wind one layer
Layer #5: Slant wind with both wire and fiber strands together
Layer #6: Slant wind with both wire and fiber strands together, in the opposite direction

Tips for Making Simple-Wound Beads

1. Review the random wind method in the Basic Techniques section, page 20, before starting to make your beads.

2. These beads have a tendency to unravel or loosen a bit if the tension on the wire and/or fiber decreases, so be sure to keep a consistent level of tension on both wires.

3. The ends of these beads, especially the narrow ones, are more fragile and should be reinforced for protection. Adding end caps is a viable solution, as is using a sealant like Dritz Fray Check to harden the ends.

4. Resist the temptation to just wind over a loop or area that's slipped out of place. If one or more of your loops slips out of position, it's best to simply unwind that loop immediately and rewind it correctly. If you try to wind over a bumpy area or loop, it can leave a bumpy area in the final bead.

5. I strongly recommend working with cotton first to help you get successful results the first time you make your beads.

6. To fill in any uneven areas in your beads, skip over several winds to prevent the bead from becoming too large, or make a wide long loop over an area.

Simple-Wound Beads

Bead #14:

Bead #15:

Bead #16:

Bead #17:

Bead #18:

General Instructions for Beads #14, 15, 16, and 17: These beads can be made extremely quickly, and they look especially appealing when made with variegated fibers. Although it can be a bit tricky at first to get the fibers to go exactly where you want them, with a little practice, you should be able to pick up this technique rather easily.

For these four beads, build your bead base on a ⅛" dowel using 26 gauge bronze or brass wire. Wind only within a ¾" to 1¼" area on the dowel, depending on how long you want your bead. At the beginning of the fourth row, add your choice of fiber strand. While holding both the strand of wire and fiber together, begin winding them on the dowel, back and forth for several rows until you have an evenly wound bead.

To create the thicker middle section of these beads, wind back and forth for a few layers in the middle area of the bead. Next, continue winding and filling in the right side to give the gradated look to the bead. Finish by winding once from right to left, filling in the left side in a gradated way as shown.

Beads #14, 15, and 16: These are all the same type bead, simply made with different fibers and wires.

Build a bead base on a ⅛" dowel using 26 gauge brass or silver wire. Wind both the fiber and the 26 gauge brass wire back and forth within a 1¼" area on the dowel to build the beads.

Bead #17: Build a bead base on a ⅛" dowel using 26 gauge copper wire. Wind within a 1¼" area on the dowel. After winding several layers of both fiber and wire together, build up the right side of the next layer. Drop the fiber strand, and build up the middle section of the bead with copper wire until it is nearly the size desired. Next, pick up the fiber strand again to build the remaining left side of the bead with both the wire and fiber strands. Finish the bead by winding two layers with the copper wire only and secure the ends.

Bead #18: Build a bead base on a ³⁄₁₆" dowel using 24 gauge brass wire. Wind within a 2" area on the dowel. Next, add a thick, nubby fiber to the wire. Continue winding both strands simultaneously to create the bead shape as shown. This bead is really just an enlarged version of the previous beads with embellished ends. To create the wire end caps, simply wind the brass wire several extra times on each end when winding the final wire layer of the bead.

Barrel Beads and the Pod Bead

The trick to making successful fiber-wire barrel beads is to make sure all the loops on the ends lie directly on top of one another, and stay there. It just takes a little additional care when you're approaching the ends.

Keep the end winds directly on top of one another.

Maintain consistency on the ends as you build the bead.

Don't let the wire and fiber slip off the end of the bead while winding.

Bead #19: Build your bead base on a ¼" dowel using 22 gauge brass wire. Wind the wire strands in a ¾" area on the dowel. Continue winding both wire and fiber strands together evenly across the entire length of the bead. Finish the ends.

Bead #20: Create this bead the same as bead #19, but wind within a 1" area.

Bead #21: The Pod Bead
Cut a 3½" length of 20 gauge copper wire. This will be the core wire on which the bead is built. Choose a heavy-ply, nubby yarn and begin winding it together with a 26 gauge rust-colored Artistic Wire for about 2¾" on the core wire. Continue winding to completion, tapering the ends as shown. Make decorative loops with the ends of the core wire to finish.

Making glued fiber-wire beads is basically foolproof. The fiber strand is wound tightly on a core wire that has glue on it. The resulting wiber can then be bent and manipulated in a variety of ways to create different kinds of fiber-wire beads.

One of the disadvantages to making these beads is that winding them on the core wires can be tedious, as well as a bit messy. The main design advantage to glued beads is that no metal shows through on the final bead.

General Instructions:

1. Refer to the individual bead instructions to determine the length of the wire needed to make the bead. This length will be the core wire. After making a few of these beads, you should be able to quickly determine core wire lengths on your own.

2. Leave the first inch or so of the core wire bare. Hold it firmly with one hand, and gently apply glue to the next several inches of that core wire. Be sure to apply the glue all the way around the wire.

3. Hold the ends of the fiber and core wire threads together. Begin straight winding the fiber around the core wire.

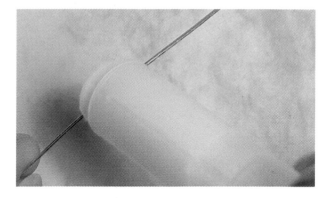

4. Continue applying glue along the core wire and winding the fiber until the core wire is wound with fiber an inch short of the end. Add a slightly heavier coating of fabric glue at the ends to prevent unwinding. This completed wiber is then wound around dowels to form the beads.

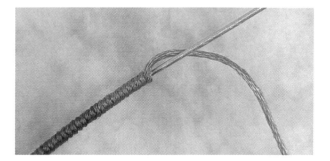

Tips for Making Glued Beads

1. Leave at least an inch or more of core wire before beginning to wind the fiber.

2. As you wind the fiber around the wire, it's very important to gently push the wound loops of thread together to ensure a tightly wound wiber.

3. Go easy on the glue. If you use too much glue, it will ooze out between the fibers as you wind them. I recommend using a glue stick for speed and control. If you have the time, use a good fabric glue like Sobo to ensure a lasting piece.

4. Allow the glue to set and dry before making beads out of these wibers. Depending on the glue you choose, a little testing here is worth the effort.

5. Be sure to straighten out your wiber before coiling it around a dowel.

6. There are two important things to remember about a core wire: First, it needs to be a thin enough gauge wire to easily wind around another wire. Second, a core wire needs to be strong enough to withstand winding fiber around it.

7. If you choose a nubby or irregular fiber or yarn, when you coil it into a bead, the nubby areas can prevent the coils from fitting together tightly.

8. Twisting the ends of the fibers clockwise between your thumb and forefinger will secure the ends. Beware: Any dirt on your fingers (often unseen) will show up in this process and darken the ends of your wibers. Wash well before you try this.

Glued Beads

Bead #22:

Bead #23:

Bead #24:

Bead #25:

Bead #26:

Bead #22: Cut 8" of 22 gauge copper for the bead core wire. Apply glue to several inches at the beginning of this wire and start straight winding a metallic thread tightly on the core wire. Continue until the core wire is wound with fiber a ½" short of the end. Trim and secure both ends. Next, wind this wiber around a ³⁄₁₆" dowel, folding the end wires into the inside of the bead to finish.

Bead #23: Proceed as with Bead #22, except cut 6" of 22 gauge copper for the core wire and use a multicolored cotton yarn. Wind the completed wiber on a ³⁄₁₆" dowel and then screw back the ends of the bead slightly.

Bead #24: Wind a multicolored embroidery floss on a 12" length of 20 gauge copper wire and secure the ends. Wind that wiber (keeping individual loops closely together) on a small Popsicle® stick until all of the wiber is used. Be sure to wind somewhat loosely so the bead will come off the stick. To finish, tuck the ends inside the bead.

Bead #25: This bead was built by winding a long wiber around a 1" wide metal ruler. It's really an enlarged version of bead #24. Here's how to make it: Cut 2½ to 3 feet of 18 gauge copper for your core wire, and then glue an aqua/beige embroidery floss on it. Secure the ends, and wind this wiber around a small metal ruler or equivalent tool.

There's a natural torque effect when wire is wound around certain shaped objects that causes the wound wire to twist naturally when removed. Square and octagon shapes produce a similar effect, although straight wire works better on those shapes than wibers do because the fiber tends to soften the look of the edges.

Bead #26: Cut a 15" length of 22 gauge copper for the core wire. Straight wind an autumnal-colored embroidery floss along the entire length, leaving roughly ½" of bare wire on both ends. Secure the fiber ends and begin straight winding 28 gauge copper wire randomly along the wiber. Leave at least ⅛" between loops, and about every inch or so, wind four or more loops close together. Straight wind a few inches of the 28 gauge copper on the bare metal ends of the wiber to add the coiled, decorative ends.

Straight wind this entire wiber on a ¼" dowel. Remove the bead from the dowel, and insert a ⅛" dowel. Wind the end wires around it. Screw back the bead a bit to create the shape as shown.

Trapped Beads and the Mesh Bead

Trapping fiber inside wire provides the greatest amount of protection for your wibers, while creating a very attractive look. Trapping fibers or fiber beads inside wire or end caps also adds considerable stability and added durability to a bead or jewelry piece.

Bead #27: This bead uses a multicolored, heavy wool yarn. The bead is built on a ¼" dowel with 22 gauge brass wire. Start by building a bead base (page 56), and wind the wool strand alone for several layers. Wind the brass wire several times; wind it flush up against one end of the bead first, and then wind it over the wool bead once. When you reach the other side of the bead, again wind several layers of brass flush up against one end, and then wind the wire back over the wool bead. Finish with a few back and forth layers of the brass. Make sure to wind several random loops on the ends to create the capped effect.

Combining slightly heavier-gauge wires with thicker fibers creates bigger, more substantial looking fiber-wire beads.

Bead #27:

Bead 28: The Mesh Bead

This bead was created with 24 gauge brass and a wide, hand-dyed mesh

Bead #28:

from a specialty knitting shop. First, build a bead base (page 56) on a ⅛" dowel. Next, cut off roughly ½" of foam from a small hair roller. Insert the wire bead base (while still on the dowel) into the hole in the center of the foam, and bind both sides of the foam with 26 gauge copper wire.

Wind the mesh around the foam several times, pulling on it to compress the foam and shape the bead.

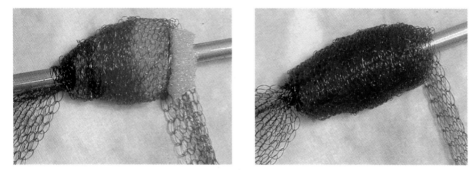

When the bead is complete, slide it off the dowel, and insert a 1½" core wire of 18 gauge copper. Add end caps by slipping them right on the ends of the core wire. The end caps protect and control the ends of the mesh nicely. Make loops on the ends of the core wire and you're done. This is a very lightweight bead.

9 *Tear Drop Necklace*

The task for this piece was to see if it was possible to design some jewelry using the beautiful glass center bead. I decided to try creating a couple fiber-wire beads with reverse colors, essentially mirroring the classic elegance of that center bead. The result demonstrates the design versatility of fiber-wire beads.

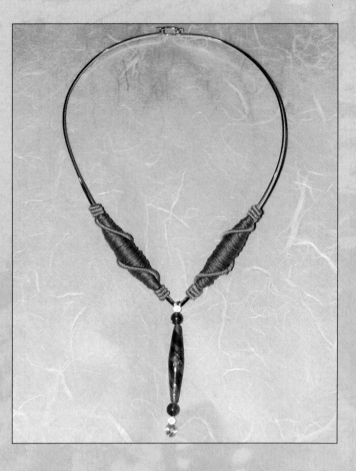

MATERIALS:

- Sterling silver neckpiece and bail
- 1 small skein each of purple and aqua embroidery floss
- 1 small spool of 20 gauge copper wire
- 1 small spool of 24 gauge copper wire
- Beads as shown
- Wire cutters, flat-nose pliers, scissors, FiberGard, Dritz Fray Check, Sobo fabric glue, sandpaper

1. Starting near the bottom on one side of the sterling silver neckpiece, build a 1¾" bead base with 24 gauge copper wire. Begin random winding purple embroidery floss for the first few layers. Follow the pattern in Basic Techniques (page 21) to build the remainder of this bead.

2. Cut a 12" length of 20 gauge copper wire (you will need to adjust this length depending on your own neck and bead size), and sand the edges. Apply glue, and tightly straight wind aqua embroidery floss onto the wire. Wind this wiber three times around the bottom of the purple bead; wind once around the purple bead itself.

3. Finish by winding the remaining aqua wiber around the neck ring on top of the purple bead.

4. Repeat for the second bead.

5. Place the center bead on a head pin and make a loop on the top.

6. Open the bail and hook it onto the loop of the head pin with the glass center bead. Then hook the other end of the bail onto the neckpiece.

These earrings are made by gluing fiber directly on aluminum "beads," purchased at an electronics store. These are simple-wound beads using a short, fuzzy, multicolored fiber and colored wire.

Once the fiber is securely glued, 24 gauge non-tarnish brass wire is wound on top.

These are extremely quick and easy to make, especially for either the beginner or simply the impatient. I'd advise paying particular attention to the ends on these beads because of their tendency to unravel.

MATERIALS:

- A short-stranded fuzzy fiber in orange, lavender, celery, or multicolored
- 24 gauge Artistic Wire non-tarnish brass
- Additional beads as needed in orange, purple, gold

- 2 brass head pins
- 2 small gold circle earrings
- Needle-nose pliers, wire cutters, scissors, Sobo fabric glue, FiberGard

1. Glue the first layer of fuzzy fiber on the aluminum beads.

2. Random wind the two remaining layers around the aluminum bead using both brass wire and fiber together like a simple-wound bead (page 56).

3. Seal the ends with Dritz Fray Check. Let dry.

4. Assemble all beads on a long head pin as shown. Add earring findings to finish (page 16).

11

Ethnic Necklace

After making so many individual fiber-wire beads with all their tiny intricacies, I couldn't help but wonder if there wasn't another, perhaps faster, way of making the beads. The simple-wound technique offered the strong appeal of not having to make a wiber first, and lent itself nicely to the following project.

After some quick experiments, it was clear that several simple-wound beads could be built in a row on a long core wire *without* cutting the wire or fiber. A necklace was a good choice for implementing and enlarging this technique. Since this necklace involves repetitive winding, you may want to work on it in a few separate sittings.

MATERIALS:

- 1 skein of a nubby multicolored magenta/aqua/black fiber
- 1 spool of 26 gauge Artistic Wire non-tarnish brass
- 12" to 14" of 12 gauge copper wire

- Small wire cutters, needle-nose pliers, flat-nose pliers, needle file, FiberGard, Dritz Fray Check, sandpaper

1. Cut a length of about 12" to 14" of 12 gauge copper wire. Tie one end of the nubby fiber about 2" from one end of the wire.

2. Begin winding the fiber firmly along the entire length of the wire, keep the loops close together and stop 2" before reaching the end. Gently form the wire into a circle to approximately fit your own neck size. (See Single Bead Neck Ring, page 40).

4. Attach the 26 gauge brass wire to one end of the necklace and begin winding along the entire length of the necklace, winding the brass "beads" on top of the fiber as you go. Make the brass "beads" by simply winding the wire several times within small areas in between the fiber "beads" and in the middle of the center fiber bead, as shown. Don't cut the wire between beads.

3. Start winding the fiber back in the opposite direction, stopping at 2" intervals to wind the individual beads. Make the "beads" along the core wire just like you'd make simple-wound beads (page 56) without cutting the fiber.

5. Wind back in the opposite direction with the brass wire once or twice to complete the necklace, and tie off the brass wire. After adjusting the necklace to your own neck, make a hook and loop on the ends of the core wire. Cut off the excess wire, and file and sand the end.

6. Apply Fray Check to the ends and let dry. Seal with FiberGard to finish.

Ethnic Bracelets

With a successful simple-wound necklace in hand, I knew the technique would translate well into bracelets.

These bracelets are both made in much the same way as the Ethnic Necklace by winding fiber and wire back and forth on a long core wire or around a pre-made bangle. The exception is that no "beads" are formed while winding the bracelets.

MATERIALS:

For Gold and Black Bracelet
- Black/gold fiber
- 26 gauge Artistic Wire non-tarnish brass
- Solid metal bangle
- FiberGard

For Magenta Bracelet
- Magenta multicolored nubby fiber
- 26 gauge Artistic Wire non-tarnish brass
- 12 gauge copper wire (to form the bracelet)
- 2 brass end caps
- E-6000 glue

1. Wind fiber and 26 gauge wire around either a pre-made metal bangle for the Gold and Black Bracelet or a core wire for the Magenta Bracelet. The length of the core wire for the Magenta Bracelet will vary a bit, depending on your own wrist size and how large you want the bracelet to be. You'll likely need a minimum of 7" to 8", and then you can custom adjust the size from there. Remember to add an extra inch to the core wire to help compensate for the fiber on the inside of the bracelet.

2. To finish the Magenta Bracelet, random wind brass wire heavily near the bracelet ends, apply E-6000 glue lightly to both ends of the wire and the inside of the end caps.

Fiber-Wire Bead Earrings

Fiber-wire beads lend themselves very well to any number of different kinds of earrings. If you're skilled at wire work, you may choose to make your own earring findings to go with your beads. If not, purchasing findings may be an easier option. Metalsmith, Pam Chott, designed BEADifferent™ Findings, a reusable jewelry system for designer beads, for just that reason. I used her findings with a few of my favorite fiber-wire beads and not only found them simple to assemble but a great enhancement to my beads.

This easy system is composed of a metal loop, a "Y" shaped key, and a French earring wire.

MATERIALS:

- Two matching fiber-wire beads
- BEADifferent Findings

1. Insert one leg of a "y" shaped piece (key) into the loop. Rotate the "y" into position with the long section of the "y" at the top and inside the loop, so the "y" appears to "ride in the saddle" at the bottom of the loop. The key will hold your bead(s) on the loop, and together they form the shaft that will fit inside the holes of the beads.

2. With your left hand, hold the two legs of the key at the bottom of the loop as you fit the desired bead over the top of the loop and down against the key. The top end of the loop should extend only enough to allow the earring to swing naturally (1/8" or less). Insert the point of the French earring wire into the top end of the loop, above the bead.

3. Continue to slide the French earring wire through the opening in the loop end until the loop end rests in the tight curve of the French wire. Grasp the larger curve of the French earring wire, and allow the assembled loop and bead to drop into position.

Chapter Five

Crocheting with Fiber and Wire

Crocheting, as a mature and popular fiber art, offers considerable potential when combined with wire. Metalsmiths and craftspeople have often demonstrated how easily wire can be adapted to crochet techniques, and artists have been applying wire to woven techniques for years. Why not fiber wire?

In this chapter, we'll explore some new possibilities for working with wire, fiber, and crochet techniques. Crocheting with chains extends some intriguing choices for fast gratification, while crocheted fiber-wire strands offer some unusual challenges for the experienced crochet artist.

All crafts and techniques have their limitations, and crocheting with wire is no exception. It takes wrist strength to pull those wires through, which can be no small deterrent. Crocheting *onto* wire with fiber solves that problem.

Crocheting onto wire also allows you the option of moving the crocheted fiber up or down the wire. You can pack it or stretch it out, easily varying the woven quality and appearance.

The addition of this stabilizing element opens the door for innumerable creative and inventive construction possibilities.

Whether you choose to make your own or use pre-made chains, crocheting fiber into chains offers some very appealing design possibilities. It's also a relatively easy way of beginning to work with fiber and wire together. Crocheting into chains incorporates the dimension of color with all its added vitality and allows you to create a complex-looking jewelry piece in very little time.

While there are many chain styles to choose from, starting with flat chain allows you to get used to working with chains. By simply altering the fiber, color, and crochet technique, you can potentially produce a wide and diversely-styled variety of jewelry.

You can crochet directly into a single chain to add your choice of fiber, or you can crochet two pieces of chain together to create a more complex-looking piece of jewelry. Either way, crocheting into chains offers some intriguing design possibilities.

General Instructions:

Crocheting into a Single Chain

1. Decide which side of the chain you'll be working on—inside or outside. Tie the fiber on the top most link of the chain, and insert the crochet hook.

2. Crochet two or more stitches into each link. Depending on the chain you use, I'd suggest testing a different number of stitches in a few links to help gauge the overall crochet pattern.

Crocheting Two Chains Together

1. Choose a chain necklace to be made into a bracelet. Fold the chain in half and lay the two sides flush to one another, making sure that all links are aligned. Tie the fiber to the top most part of the first loop on the chain.

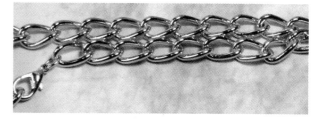

2. Insert the crochet hook under and through the two inside links at the beginning of the chain.

3. Pull the fiber strand through both inside links and single crochet.

4. Single crochet two or more stitches into the same two links, depending on the look you want and the size of the link hole. Again, the number of stitches per link will depend on both the size of the fiber used and the size of the link hole.

Tips for Crocheting into Chains

1. Flat chains are the easiest kind to use.

2. When choosing your chain, make sure the holes in the chain are large enough to work your crochet needle through.

3. Be sure to crochet tightly enough to bind the chain links together but loosely enough to allow the chain to lay flat on completion. Test the first two or three links after you've crocheted them together to be sure that they'll lay flat once you've finished.

4. Keep the size of the fiber or the number of stitches you use in good proportion to the size of the chain. For example, if you have a heavy chain, use a heavier fiber with fewer stitches per link. If you use a thinner fiber, make more stitches to add sufficient fiber per link. It's very important to make sure the fiber is strong enough to keep the two parts of the chain together once crocheted.

5. The most difficult thing about crocheting into chains is keeping the links properly aligned while working on the chain. This will vary greatly depending on the type of chain you use. Chains are "slippery" but once you've successfully secured the initial links, crocheting the remainder of the piece should be relatively easy.

6. Before you begin, decide which side of the chain you'll be working on, and stick with it.

I used an inexpensive opera length chain necklace for this bracelet. The challenge was to see if I could successfully translate the necklace into an effective bracelet by crocheting it together without removing the clasp.

I chose the thin-gauge variegated metallic thread to enhance the gunmetal color of the chain and to add a subtle touch of sparkle and color. The double links on this chain were attractive, and I wanted them to show through without too much fiber covering them. To give a stronger appearance to the bracelet, I used a thin black cotton thread and bead-crocheted the gunmetal beads on the top of the original crochet work.

MATERIALS:

- 13" double link flat chain necklace
- 1 small skein of black/blue/copper thread
- 1 small skein of black cotton thread

- 24 small gunmetal beads
- Size F crochet hook
- Dritz Fray Check, Sobo fabric glue, scissors

1. Fold the double link flat chain necklace in half. Use the size F crochet hook to crochet three single crochet stitches of the black/blue/copper thread into the center of each pair of links. Tie off the end, seal with Fray Check, and carefully feed the end back into the crochet.

2. String 24 small gunmetal beads on the black cotton thread.

3. Crochet into both top chevrons of each of the first row of stitches. Before you do the final pull through on each stitch, pull up a bead and crochet it in. Tie off the ends, and seal with Fray Check to finish.

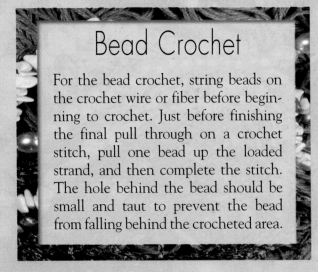

Bead Crochet

For the bead crochet, string beads on the crochet wire or fiber before beginning to crochet. Just before finishing the final pull through on a crochet stitch, pull one bead up the loaded strand, and then complete the stitch. The hole behind the bead should be small and taut to prevent the bead from falling behind the crocheted area.

This is a quick project that demonstrates the ease of crocheting into a chain. This classic necklace can be worn as an everyday, casual piece. Altering the crochet technique, the number of stitches, and the type and color of the fiber can quickly and easily change the style of the necklace, if desired.

- 1 skein thin aqua/purple yarn
- 1 small skein green boucle
- 15" flat link gold chain necklace

- Size F and 1 crochet needles
- Dritz Fray Check, Sobo glue, FiberGard

1. Using aqua/purple yarn, crochet two single stitches into each of the links of the gold chain necklace.

2. To create the finished effect, single crochet with green boucle for the second row in the following manner:

    a. Single crochet for the length of four chain links, and then do three chain stitches.

    b. Pull that small chain length up to the top of the fifth link, and single crochet three times into it.

3. Do three more chain stitches, and pull that chain stitch section down. Skip over three of the first row stitches, and single crochet again for the length of four chain links. Repeat this pattern three times to complete one side of the necklace.

4. Match up the sides of the necklace, and mark where you'll make the first scallop for the second side.

5. Repeat steps #2 and #3 for the second side of the necklace. Seal the ends with Fray Check and a tiny bit of Sobo fabric glue. When dry, spray with FiberGard, and tuck in the ends.

16

Regal Necklace

It was intriguing to see how well crocheting into chains would work with very heavy chain. This project is a good example of how to choose the right fiber to correlate with chain density. I'd recently found small cards of velvet fiber in a needlework store, and I felt velvet would provide an interesting contrast to the twisted wire chain. It would also be strong yet soft enough to support the two chains together while still allowing the completed chain to easily lay flat. The elegance of velvet coordinates well with the antiqued chain for a contemporary Victorian look. The small, faceted beads were chosen to enhance that style.

- 12" length double-twisted wire chain
- 1 small spool of 26 gauge silver wire
- Size F crochet hook
- Several feet of thin lavender velvet cord
- 30 to 40 purple dyed quartz beads

- 18 small iridescent black/blue/purple faceted beads
- Sterling end caps and S clasp
- Black antique solution
- Needle-nose pliers

1. Fold the double-twisted wire chain in half, and lay the two halves side-by-side. Use the size F crochet hook to single crochet once with lavender velvet cord into all links.

2. Flip the crocheted chain over. This is the side the beads will be attached to.

3. String all beads on 26 gauge silver wire as shown.

4. Using the black antique solution, antique roughly 4 feet of the 26 gauge silver wire (see Antique Wire, page 29). Fold the wire in half, and twist it tightly.

5. To attach the bead strand, wind the twisted wire around it and through the center of the chain. Continue until you have attached the entire center of the strand of beads to the chain. Twist and then tuck the end wires into the back. Add the sterling end caps and S clasp to finish.

Finally, as I was preparing to add the bead strand, I realized the chain also could have been made into a handsome and hefty bracelet.

Crocheting onto thin-gauge wire creates another thicker and more substantial type of wiber. The wire is covered by the fiber, providing an unseen thin metal base that adds new-found strength and pliability to crochet work. Since the wire is thin-gauge, it's relatively easy to bend and crochet around it. You can also create wider wibers by adding more rows of crochet, with or without adding wire. Changing fibers with different textures provides interesting variables and options as well. This new dimension adds the promise of amazing structural possibilities to the aged craft of crochet.

3. Finish the rest of the stitch as usual.

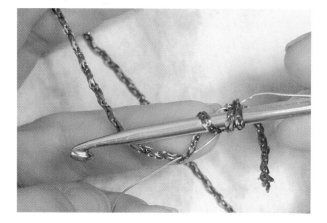

General Instructions:

1. Tie both ends of your fiber and wire together, leaving a small loop.

2. Insert the crochet hook into that loop. Put the crochet hook *under* the wire and pull the fiber under it and slightly up.

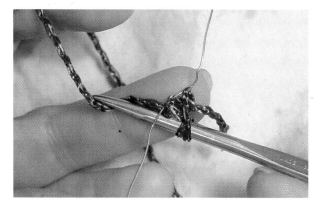

Using Wire In Multiple-Row Crochets

Just as you generally chain stitch before turning to start another row of crochet, make sure to chain stitch onto the wire. Otherwise you'll have wire showing on all of the ends of the final crocheted piece.

Tips for Crocheting onto Wire

1. Choose a thin-gauge wire to begin learning this technique. Copper wire is fairly soft and will be easy to manipulate if you use 26 gauge. Once you've mastered crocheting onto thin-gauge wires, working with a heavier-gauge wire should be much easier.

2. If you plan to do two or more rows of crocheting onto wire, make sure to bend the wire up to the next row.

3. Don't crochet the wire; crochet around it. The wire should remain straight as you continue to work the crochet.

4. Be careful. While the thinner gauge wires are easier to manipulate, they also can be problematic to crochet onto since they move around so freely. For example, 28 and 30 gauge wires will bend easily as you crochet; this makes it hard not to crochet with both the wire and the fiber.

Crocheting with Fiber and Wire

17

Crocheted Wiber Braid Neckpiece

Option 1

For this necklace, I started with the idea that crocheted wibers would integrate nicely into a braided neckpiece. As the sample braid began to unfold, I noticed that the ends of the ribbon used in the wibers began to separate. To solve this problem, I crocheted some green and black boucle to the sides of each original wiber, which also added a little more texture to the piece.

Working on the theory that I'd want to see some metal for contrast and physical weight, as one option I added some heavy gauge sterling wire into the piece, one strand running through the center to mimic the movement of the braided wiber.

As a second option, I added some small silver ball chain to the center area of the braid. The wire brought strong contrast and added to the overall strength and drama of the piece.

MATERIALS:

- 1 skein of black/green/purple ribbon fiber
- 1 small skein of black and green boucle
- 1 small skein of purple cotton fiber
- 2 medium-sized glossy black cords
- 1 small matte black cord
- 1 spool of 24 gauge copper wire

- 12" to 14" of 14 gauge sterling silver wire or 5 feet of small silver ball chain
- Sterling silver end caps, hook, and clasp
- Dritz Fray Check, Sobo glue, metal polishing cloth, sandpapers, wire cutters, needle file, scissors

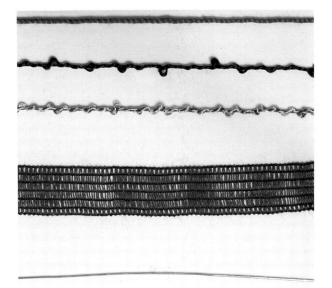

Fibers and wire to make the wibers.

1. Single crochet the multicolored ribbon fiber on 24 gauge copper wire for 2½ feet. Repeat for the second wiber.

2. Using a slightly lighter shade of green boucle, single crochet along one side of one wiber. Repeat with black boucle on the remaining side of the wiber.

3. For the second wiber, single crochet with purple cotton fiber along both sides.

The completed wibers.

4. Choose one style of the braid, and assemble the strands as shown.

Strands for option 1, the sterling wire braid:

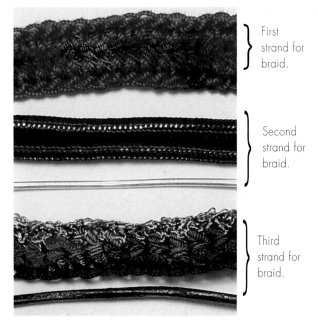

First strand for braid.

Second strand for braid.

Third strand for braid.

Strands for option 2, the ball chain braid:

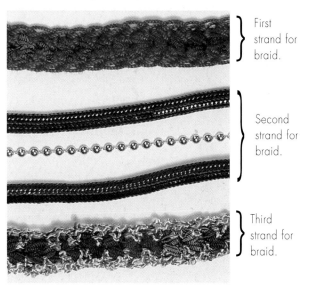

First strand for braid.

Second strand for braid.

Third strand for braid.

Crocheting with Fiber and Wire

5. For either style, you will be doing a three-strand braid.

    a. For the sterling wire style, leave the wire out of the initial braid and consider the two black cords the center strand of the braid. Finish the braid, and then carefully weave in the sterling wire, making wavy bends in it with your thumb and forefinger.

    b. For the ball chain, bind the chain to the two black cords at 1" and ½" intervals with silver wire as shown.

6. Once the braid is completed, trim the excess, and seal with Dritz Fray Check. Add the end caps and clasp to finish.

Consider this the center strand and braid the entire piece together.

Option 2

18

Gold and Black Crocheted Cuff Bracelet

Crocheting onto wire requires little more physical effort than simple crocheting, yet it creates a woven surface with a wire support that offers a number of new possibilities for fiber-wire crochet work. Crocheting directly onto a wire frame provides the added structural support to give the piece more durability. While initially a bit challenging to work the crochet hook into those small spaces, the results make it well worth the effort.

MATERIALS:

- 1 skein of black/gold metallic ribbon
- 1 spool of 26 gauge brass wire
- 1 spool of 16 gauge brass wire
- 3" of thin gauge black steel wire
- Size F crochet hook
- Size 1 crochet hook

- Black ceramic donut
- Gold button
- 2" round PVC pipe or a soup can
- Vice
- Dowel
- Dritz Fray Check, FiberGard

1. Cut an 18" length of 16 gauge brass wire. Fold it in half, and use a vice and dowel to twist it together tightly.

2. Fold that twisted strand in half around a 2" PVC pipe or a soup can to form one end of the cuff.

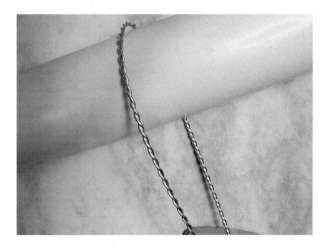

3. Use the PVC pipe or soup can to start molding the cuff into shape, curving the second end like the first.

4. Continue forming the cuff, adjusting the size to your own wrist.

5. Separate the two wires on each end.

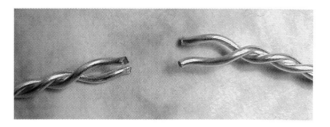

6. Fit the ends tightly into one another.

7. Trim, file, and sand all ends. Firmly bind them together with 26 gauge brass wire. Be careful not to over wind too much wire, or a visible lump will show in your final cuff.

8. Begin single crocheting *around* one end of the cuff by inserting the size F hook under the wire frame and pulling the fiber under it and up. The cuff frame is crocheted with fiber *only*.

9. Crochet in this fashion all the way around the cuff frame.

10. Using the size 1 crochet hook, begin filling in the center area of the cuff by single crocheting with both the black/gold metallic ribbon and 26 gauge brass wire. Crochet from top to bottom starting at one end of the cuff and be sure to crochet into both the top and bottom areas from the original row on the frame.

11. Continue as above until the entire cuff is crocheted. If you run out of room for a final row, sew the two crocheted areas together with a black thread.

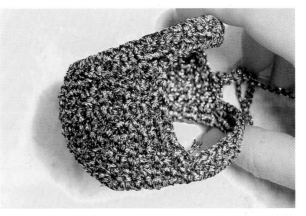

One of the true advantages to crocheting with wire is that it's possible to move or shift the position of a stitch and have it stay there because of the wire underbody. As you work this project, you will need to make adjustments in stitches for your own cuff size but it is most advantageous to be able to widen or scrunch the stitches where needed.

12. Run thin-gauge black steel wire through the shank in a gold button, and insert it into the ceramic donut hole through the crochet, centering both on the cuff. To finish the attachment, pull the steel wire over to the front of the cuff, wind around the base of the donut, and press down.

Crocheting with Fiber and Wire

19

Crocheted Wiber Cuff Bracelet

One of the primary advantages of crocheted wibers is that their density can vary greatly depending on the size of the fiber used. Unlike standard crocheting with yarns, you can also form finished pieces. Since several fiber strands can be crocheted together to create a single wiber, crocheted wibers offer the opportunity to create some potentially interesting color palettes. Dense or large wibers can make it easy to quickly fill in any area in a jewelry piece as well.

This is a great beginning project for a crocheter who wants to make jewelry but isn't familiar or comfortable working with wire.

- 2 sterling silver bangle bracelets
- Medium-sized decorative metal button
- 1 foot of 22 gauge silver wire
- 1 small spool 26 gauge silver wire
- Size F crochet hook

- 1 skein of a black mesh fiber
- 1 skein of a 3-ply black/silver fiber
- Needle-nose pliers, scissors, Dritz Fray Check, FiberGard

1. Position one of the two bangles inside the other one, forming a kind of butterfly structure. Make sure both sides are equal size, and use 22 gauge silver wire to bind each side of the structure where the two bangles crisscross. Adjust the bracelet to your own wrist, leaving extra room fro the black mesh fiber. Tuck in the wire ends.

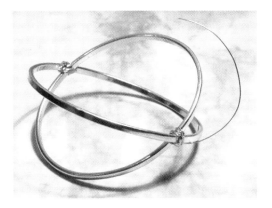

2. Using the size F crochet hook, single crochet 3 feet of the black/silver fiber onto 26 gauge silver wire to create the wiber.

The completed wiber.

3. Tightly wind one end of the wiber on the bottom-most area closest to the bound crisscross. Pull the wiber up firmly, and loop it around the top of the upper bangle in a beginning figure 8 pattern.

4. Continue winding the wiber in the figure 8 pattern until one side is completed. Compress and pack the wiber tightly as you wind.

5. Repeat #2 and #3 for the second side of the bracelet. Carefully wind the wiber over the crisscross sections.

6. Seal the ends with Fray check, and tuck them inside.

7. Spray with FiberGard. Sew the metal button on one side of the bracelet to finish.

As I began conceptualizing this chapter on crochet, I have to admit that I had some trepidation. I'd never really gotten into the more creative aspects of crochet.

Mulling this over, I thought of Lydia F. Borin. Lydia specializes in bead crochet, and we'd had some exchanges in the past about our mutual interest in fiber and wire. I thought I could do some interesting, if basic, things with wire and fiber crochet but I knew Lydia could do knock 'em dead things with beads and fiber. I decided to approach her.

In the course of our initial conversation, we hit on Bead Crocheted Beads as an interesting project option. While I could certainly use crocheted wibers to make beads as I'd done with the other kinds of wibers, I liked the idea of a fresh, different approach to crocheted beads and thought it would add a great new dimension to the chapter. Lydia delivered in spades.

The following beads and bead crocheted necklaces are the result of her enthusiasm and weeks of experimentation. As I expected, the pieces are indeed knock 'em dead, and I'm delighted and grateful to be able to include them here.

Adding Beads to Crochet

An excerpt from the book *Beadwrangler's Hands on Crochet with Beads and Fiber* by Lydia F. Borin:

Beads can be added to chain stitches, single crochet, double crochet, and half double crochet. They can be added before or after *any* yarnover in a stitch. More than one bead can be added in a stitch. Beads can be added before or after *every* yarnover in a stitch. Make a sampler of all bead placements in stitches for reference.

For all bead stitches: As soon as you add a bead, give the thread a tug, pulling the hook taut so the bead sits on the outside of the crochet piece and does not pull through to the inside, which is facing you. Beads pull through if the loops behind them are too big. Smaller hooks make smaller loops that keep the beads in place.

For single crochet: String some beads on crochet thread. Then make a group of single crochet stitches in a circle. (See the single crochet circle illustration.) Put the crochet hook through the next stitch for a single crochet, pull up the nearest bead on the thread, and push it snug against the crocheted stitches. Yo behind the bead and pull a loop through. (See the left and right handed bead single crochet illustrations.) Yo again and draw through both loops on the hook. The bead single crochet is complete, and the bead is attached. Continue until finished. Use this bead placement for all the projects requiring bead single crochet stitches. Beads can also be placed on after the first yo of a single crochet.

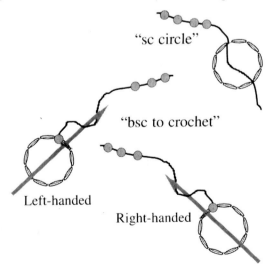

"sc circle"

"bsc to crochet"

Left-handed

Right-handed

Patterned Bead Crocheted Beads

by Lydia F. Borin, The Beadwrangler

Bead Size Examples: All these bead combinations work for both beads. The larger the beads used, the heavier and bigger the beaded bead will be. Choose one of these examples, or try other bead sizes and shapes. Delicas and 14/0 beads look best on thinner thread (e.g. 100wt. polyester).

- 3 size 8/0 and 1 size 6/0
- 3 size 11/0 and 1 size 8/0 seed bead
- 3 size 11/0 and 1 size 8/0 hex bead
- 3 size 9/0 cuts and 1 gemstone chip
- 3 Delicas and 1 size 9/0, 10/0, or 11/0
- 3 size 14/0 Japanese beads and 1 Delica

Materials:

- Choose beads from bead size examples
- YLI Jean Stitch thread (substitutes: Cebelia #30/DMC or Anchor #12 pearl cotton)
- #7 or #8 embroidery needles
- Medium twisted wire needles
- #9/1.40mm steel crochet hook
- Scissors

General Instructions:

1. Pre-string the beads on the crochet thread in color order. The last bead you string is the first bead you will crochet. Each bead color sequence is listed across from the round in which it is worked.

2. Pull up the beads for a round, and keep them separate from the rest of the strung beads. Once you have crocheted the beads for that round, pull up the beads for the next round. This is an easy method to keep up with the correct number of beads for each round.

3. Work in a continuous spiral, and don't join the rounds with a slip stitch. Take the hook under both stitch halves for all decrease stitches and those stitches in which new thread is attached. Take the hook under the back half of all other stitches for both beads and ropes. If you work very loose, take the hook under both stitch halves for all projects.

4. When you run out of beads, fasten off, leaving a 3" tail thread. String beads again, continuing with the bead color sequence. Make a slipknot in the thread with strung beads. Take the hook through the last stitch worked, from the wrong side to the right side, put the slip knot on the hook, and bring it through that stitch. Begin crocheting in the next stitch. If need be, use a needle to stitch in the loose fastened off thread before continuing with new thread. However, do not stitch over the stitches in the current round.

Standard USA Abbreviations:

ch   chain
sc   single crochet
sk   skip
rep   repeat
st(s)   stitch(es)
sl st   slip stitch
yo   yarnover

Standard Bead Crochet Abbreviation:

bsc   bead single crochet

Abbreviations used in the following projects:

c1 bead color #1
c2 bead color #2 (always the odd/larger bead)
c3 bead color #3
c4 bead color #4

A number added in front of the "c" indicates how many beads of that color will be added. Example: c3 means one bead color #3; 2c3 means two beads color #3.

The second c2 bead in each round can be different than the first c2 bead in each round. Two different beads for c2 in a round may flatten the appearance on both sides of the bead crocheted bead. Two same type c2 beads in each round form a twisted bead crocheted bead.

Bead #29: The Malana—Short Bead

The example bead is worked with the first c2 as a gemstone chip and the second c2 as an 8/0 hex bead, making both bead sides flatten out in shape. The beginning and ending rounds are worked in 9/0 size cut beads. Use the smaller beads for the beginning and ending rounds, not 8/0 or larger beads. Begin by ch6 and join with a sl st to form a ring.

Pattern Round and Bead Color

Round 1: 6c1, c3, or c4; 1bsc in each st around (6sts) **Round 2:** c1, c2, 2c3, c1, c2, 2c3, c4; *1bsc in 1 st, 2bsc in the next st, * repeat from * around (9sts) **Round 3:** c1, c2, 2c3, c1, c2, 2c3, c4; 1bsc in each st around (9sts) **Round 4:** c1, c2, 2c3, 2c4, c1, c2, c3, 3c4; *1bsc in each next 2 sts, 2bsc in next st,* rep from * around (12sts) **Round 5:** c1, c2, 2c3, 2c4, c1, c2, c3, 3c4; 1bsc in each st around (12sts) **Round 6:** c1, c2, 3c3, 3c4, c1, c2, 2c3, 3c4; *1bsc in each next 3 sts, 2bsc in next st, * repeat from * around (15sts) **Round 7 & 8:** c1, c2, 3c3, 3c4, c1, c2, 2c3, 3c4; 1bsc in each st around (15 sts in each 2 rnds) **Round 9:** c1, c2, 2c3, 2c4, c1, c2, c3, 3c4; *1bsc in each next 3 sts, sk next st, rep from * around (12sts) **Round 10:** c1, c2, 2c3, 2c4, c1, c2, c3, 3c4; 1bsc in each st around (12sts) **Round 11:** c1, c2, 2c3, c1, c2, 2c3, c4; *sk 1 st, 1bsc in each next 3sts, * rep from * around (9sts) **Round 12:** c1, c2, 2c3, c1, c2, 2c3, c4; 1bsc in each st around (9sts) **Round 13:** 6c1, c3, or c4; *sk 1 st, 1bsc in each next 2 sts, * rep from * around (6sts) Fasten off. Stitch in loose thread.

Patterned Bead Crocheted Beads by Lydia F. Borin, The Beadwrangler

Bead #30:
The Gamay—Long Bead

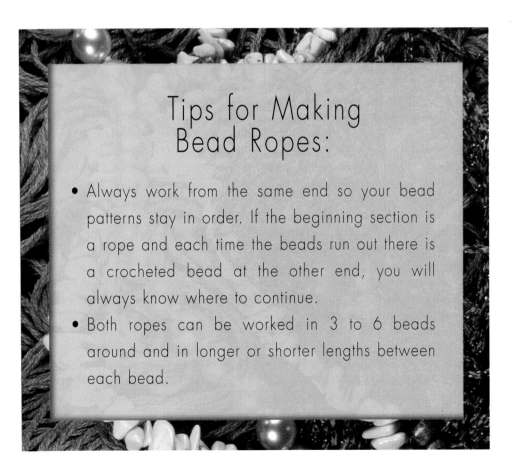

around (6sts) **Round 3:** c1, c2, 2c3, c1, c2, 2c3, c4; *1bsc in 1 st, 2bsc in the next st, * rep from * around (9sts)
Round 4: c1, c2, 2c3, c1, c2, 2c3, c4; 1bsc in each st around (9sts) **Round 5:** c1, c2, 2c3, 2c4, c1, c2, 1c3, 3c4; *1bsc in each next 2 sts, 2bsc in next st,* rep from * around (12sts) **Round 6-18:** c1, c2, 2c3, 2c4, c1, c2, 1c3, 3c4; 1bsc in each st around (12sts in each 13 rnds)
Round 19: c1, c2, 2c3, c1, c2, 2c3, c4; *sk 1 st, 1bsc in each next 3 sts, * rep from * around (9sts) **Round 20:** c1, c2, 2c3, c1, c2, 2c3, c4; 1bsc in each st around (9sts)
Round 21: 6 of c1, c3, or c4; *sk 1 st, 1bsc in each next 2 sts, * rep from * around (6sts) Fasten off.

Patterned Bead Crocheted Beads by Lydia F. Borin, The Beadwrangler

This bead is a thinner and longer variation of the Malana. Begin by ch6 and join with sl st to form a ring.

Pattern Round and Bead Colors
Round 1: 6 of c1, c3 or c4; 1bsc in each st around (6sts)
Round 2: 11/0 or 8/0 of c1, c3, or c4; 1bsc in each st

Tips for Making Bead Ropes:

- Always work from the same end so your bead patterns stay in order. If the beginning section is a rope and each time the beads run out there is a crocheted bead at the other end, you will always know where to continue.

- Both ropes can be worked in 3 to 6 beads around and in longer or shorter lengths between each bead.

20

Malana/Gamay Bead Ropes

by Lydia F. Borin, The Beadwrangler

Malana

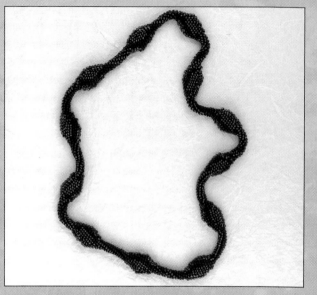

Gamay

Choose either the Gamay or the Malana bead for your rope, and use the instructions for that bead to make the bead portion of the rope. In between each bead, you will be adding a rope section. You can make a thin rope with three beads per round or a thicker rope with five beads per round. Use the same beads you used in round one of the Gamay or Malana bead pattern.

1. String the beads for the rope section first. Then string the bead color sequence. Repeat this process until you have strung enough to make five beads with a rope section between each bead.

A. Malana Rope: Work 20 rope rounds between each bead, 3 beads in each round. When finishing a rope section, increase by 2bsc in each stitch, which would be round 1 of the bead pattern, then continue. At the end of the bead pattern, *sk 1 st, 1bsc in the next st, * rep from * resulting in 3bsc per round. Work 20 rounds between each bead, 1 bead of c1, c3, and c4 in each round to add contrast between each bead.

B. Gamay Rope: Work 15 rounds between each bead, 6 beads in each round. The beads are worked with size 8/0 beads except c2,

which is a size 6/0 bead. For the rope, string 2c1, 2c3, and 2c4, repeat for 15 rounds. Then string the bead pattern. The rope will be thicker and spiral more than the Malana. It will also be much heavier in weight.

2. Crochet the rope and beads, then fasten off, string another section, attach the thread, and continue until you have the length desired.

3. To finish the Malana or Gamay Rope, join the two ends, rope at one end, and bead at the other. Use a needle to stitch the ends together. Stitch the loose fastened off thread from one end to the other. Take the needle through more of the rope above and below where the two ends join. Cut off the excess thread.

Chapter Six

Combination and Other Hybrid Techniques

learned early on, listening to my readers, that they were not only looking for inspiration or interesting projects, they were also looking for some variety and challenge. If that sounds like you, then you've come to the right chapter.

In the previous chapters, we've applied a number of simple fiber and wire techniques to create numerous, varied beads and jewelry. This chapter explores several other ways of using and combining some of those techniques.

For many months, I hunted for and accumulated a wide variety of interesting and unusual jewelry parts. Several times while mulling over this cornucopia of goodies, I found myself taking out a handful of ball chain, admiring the elegant symmetry it offered. Then I'd put it away when no immediate applications came to mind.

Every few days I'd return to the box of ball chain until I finally gave it a permanent viewing spot on my desk. I cleaned and polished it, held it up to the sun to admire its sparkle, and allowed it to play with my hand movements.

Setting it down one day, I noticed that it rather naturally took on a rope-like appearance … only better. Thinking it would be too easy to simply bind the multiple lengths together, I picked up a wiber and decided to try to figure out what the challenges would be. At the very least, I expected it to be a multiple-step process. It wasn't.

The wiber seemed to immediately grab onto the cluster of ball chain and, much to my surprise, stay there firmly. I shook it, banged it around, wore it, and tried anything I could think of to test its stability. Short of some slight loosening near the end (where I hadn't bound it), it stayed together quite nicely. Since simple solutions are a rarity, I realized that a true jewelry-making miracle had occurred. I couldn't wait to test several different versions of my new discovery.

General Instructions for Winding Wibers around Ball Chain

The three sizes of ball chain—small, medium, and large—are composed of brass or chrome, and they're available in most hardware stores. Sterling silver ball chain is available from a number of jewelry supply houses.

Small, medium, and large ball chain.

1. A ball chain rope can have any number of strands in the rope. The only difficult part about winding wibers around ball chain is that the chain is slippery and a bit hard to get started. As a result, you may want to bind the lengths together first with plain wire. Bind for three or four loops, just under where you plan to begin winding with the wiber. That way, once you've completed two or three winds with the wiber, you can easily remove the binding wire. You can also bind in this manner as you proceed to build your entire ball chain rope. Although once you get going, it shouldn't be necessary again until you reach the end.

2. Once you get started, you'll see how easily the wiber fits in the small areas between the metal balls and almost begs to be bound.

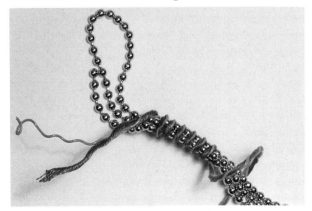

Winding a wiber to make a ball chain rope.

Black and Sterling Ball Chain Necklace

This necklace came together so smoothly it almost made itself. The first black and silver wiber I tried wound the strands of ball chain together seamlessly in less than five minutes. I already had exactly the right end caps, and during my trip to the supply store, the gray cat's eye clasp beamed up at me immediately.

Even better was watching people's faces when I showed it to them. Admiration was followed by closer examination and inevitably the question, "How DID you do that?" When I showed or explained the method, no one seemed to believe me, which confirmed exactly what I wanted to know. The technique produced an end result that looked far more complex and time consuming than it actually was.

MATERIALS:

- 1 skein black cotton fiber
- 5 feet of large silver ball chain
- 1 spool of 26 gauge fine silver wire
- 1 spool of 18 gauge sterling wire
- End caps
- Clasp

- 2 jump rings
- Pendant
- E-6000 jewelry glue
- Wire cutters, scissors, needle-nose pliers, Dritz Fray Check

1. Cut four 12" to 14" strands of large silver ball chain. Test this length on your own neck and adjust the ball chain lengths accordingly.

2. Make a 3½ foot wiber with the 26 gauge sterling wire and black fiber. Seal one end.

3. Grasp all four chains, and press them together. Begin winding the wiber around the chains 1" from the end, and continue to wind along the entire length of the ball chain.

4. Seal both ends with Dritz Fray Check, and trim any excess ball chain. Wind a new 3" strand of 18 gauge sterling wire around each end to secure it, leaving at least 2" of wire extending. Insert this wire into the end caps and make loops to finish. Attach the clasp.

Ball Chain and Opal Pendant

It's hard to resist the appeal of cascading ball chain, especially when it's combined with a bead as beautiful as this one by Susan Berkowitz.

While I was just starting to work with the ball chain, I met Susan, a polymer clay artist. I asked her if she had any beads or pendants she might be interested in contributing. This piece was inspired by the subtle elegance of her opalescent polymer clay bead.

- 1 skein of lavender fiber
- 1 spool of 22 gauge powder blue Artistic Wire
- 1 spool of 20 gauge sterling silver wire
- 4 strands of small ball chain, 3 foot long
- 5 strands of medium-sized ball chain, 3 foot long
- One gorgeous center bead
- Sterling end caps for the center bead and clasp
- Wire cutters, scissors, needle-nose pliers, large dowel

1. Use two 8-foot lengths of both the lavender fiber and the blue wire to make a 4-foot wiber for each side of this project.

2. Use the sterling silver wire to bind all nine strands of ball chain together (at 2" to 3" intervals) before you begin. Try to place the smaller ball chain strands on the inside of the bundle.

3. Begin winding the wiber at least one inch down from the ends of the ball chain, and wind down the first side for about ¼ of the total length of your chain. Repeat for the second side.

4. When you reach the end of the wiber winds on each side, cut off the excess wiber, leaving 2". Separate the fiber from the wire on that wiber and firmly wind the wire around two or three ball chain strands on the inside of the bundle.

5. To make the bail on the bead, insert 20 gauge sterling wire through the bead. Place a large dowel on the top end of the bead and wind the wire twice around the dowel. The bail you make should be large enough for the ball chain rope to fit through.

6. Bind a short length of small ball chain loosely around this bail and then secure it by winding firmly with a piece of the wiber.

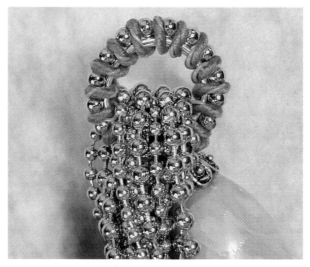

7. Finish the ends of the rope by again, separating the fiber from the wire on the wiber. Seal the fiber with Dritz Fray Check and then wind a 3" strand of 20 gauge silver wire tightly around the base.

8. Slip the end cap over this wire, cut away the remaining blue wire, and secure the cap by winding the wire twice around a small dowel.

9. Add jump rings and clasp to finish.

Brown and Leopard Jasper Necklace

This project uses crochet to create a dense fiber and wire neckpiece. By crocheting two small skeins of fiber together and then feeding thick wire through the crocheted areas, a soft but firm wire-supported neckpiece is created. Placing the wire in the center of the two skeins of fiber provides not only strength and support for the neckpiece but adds just the right touch of metal to the overall look. The yellow brass wire picks up the color of the gold bead, providing visual integration and balance to the jewelry.

MATERIALS:

- 4 brown/taupe fiber skeins
- Black boucle for crochet
- 12" to 14" of 16 gauge brass wire
- 1 spool of 20 gauge brass wire
- 1 spool of 26 gauge brass wire
- 1 spool of Taupe Artistic Wire
- Size F crochet hook

- A few black beads
- A few large gold oval beads
- 1 leopard jaspar donut bead
- 1 large leopard jaspar oval bead
- End caps
- Wire cutters, awl, needle-nose pliers, flat-nose pliers, Popsicle stick, scissors, Dritz Fray Check

1. Place two brown/taupe fiber skeins flush to one another. Use black boucle to crochet together the first two inside twists of the skeins. Single crochet three times into that twist area, and then make two chain stitches. Repeat this pattern for the remaining length of the skeins. Repeat all for the second two skeins. Leave the last few twist areas uncrocheted on the ends of each skein.

2. Place the bottom ends of two small skeins of fiber together, and bind them securely with 26 gauge brass wire.

3. Using an awl or small slender object, lift up the crocheted areas at the top of one end of the neckpiece. Feed 16 gauge brass wire throughout the entire center area of the neckpiece. Leave roughly 2" of wire loose on the ends.

4. Wind 20 gauge brass wire a few times inside and around the top of each skein, and add the end caps. Note that the end caps in this photo are different from the ones in the piece.

5. Using flat-nose pliers, make a bend in the wire. Carefully wind each of the two end wires just under the end caps. File and sand the ends, and tuck the wire in close.

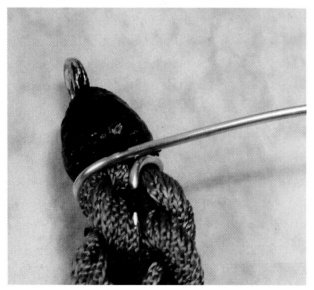

6. Using 26 gauge brass wire, loosely bind the center area of the neckpiece for additional support.

7. Place a Popsicle stick on top of the center area and wind 20 gauge brass wire around it for a few inches. Be sure to test the first few winds to make sure they'll slide off the Popsicle stick. If they get stuck, start again and wind more loosely. File and sand the end wires, and tuck them in to finish.

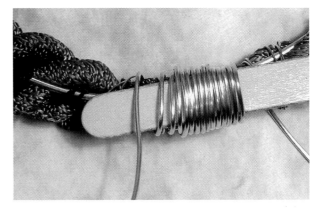

8. Assemble all beads on a long head pin as shown. Make a loop on the top. Slip the loop onto one of the center loops of the brass coil, and then close that head pin loop.

9. Seal ends with Dritz Fray Check. When dry, spray with FiberGard.

Combination and Other Hybrid Techniques

24

Octagon Bracelet

Did you know you can screw coils onto and into other things? In this project, you'll screw a coil onto a bangle bracelet and secure it with a wiber. This is a wonderful small project that produces not only a most-interesting textural effect but also a very sturdy piece of jewelry. By using the wiber to bind the coil into place, it secures the coil, stabilizes it, and makes the spacing between the coil loops even.

- Multicolored blue/aqua/green fiber
- 26 gauge sterling silver wire
- Sterling silver octagon bangle

- ¼" dowel
- Wire cutters, needle-nose pliers, scissors, Sobo fabric glue, Dritz Fray Check

Note: *It's essential that your original bangle be large enough to accommodate the addition of the fiber on the inside. Otherwise it can become too small for your wrist.*

1. Straight wind about a 4" coil of 26 gauge sterling silver wire onto a ¼" dowel. (Adjust the measurements to fit your wrist.) Stretch the coil out slightly so that there are even spaces between the loops.

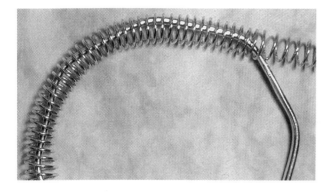

2. Wind the end of the coiled wire onto the bangle and continue turning the coil as each new loop gets twisted onto the bangle.

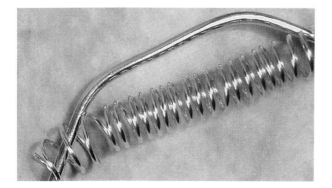

3. When the entire coil has been screwed onto the bangle, use needle-nose pliers to make small loops in both end wires and tuck them in.

4. Make a long wiber, roughly 2½ to 3 feet depending on the size of your bracelet, using the 26 gauge silver wire and the multicolored fiber. Bind the bracelet to the coil by winding the wiber in between each loop. When moving from one coil to the next, it is essential to angle the wiber *over* the next coil loop before winding into that loop.

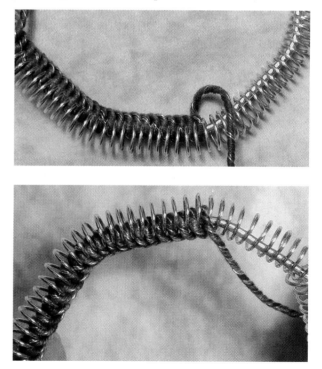

5. Seal and tuck in the ends to complete. Once finished, you can move the coil to even out the spacing, if desired.

25

Square Bracelet

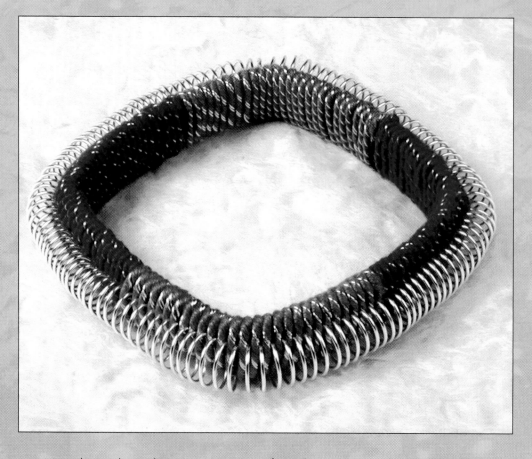

I realize that the components for doing this project aren't that readily available. It's been included here to demonstrate how easy it is to coordinate fiber-wire jewelry with wearables. Looking to accomplish that, I approached Suzanne Pineau, a knitting artist and owner of Knitting in La Jolla, early on in the project. An enthusiastic participant, Suzanne knitted this gorgeous sweater and then helped me find matching yarns to work into a color-coordinated bracelet. I'm proud to include her work here and delighted to have had her to collaborate with.

- 1 skein each of magenta, navy, pink fibers
- 1 spool of 26 gauge silver wire
- 1 spool of 26 gauge non-tarnish silver Artistic Wire
- 2 square sterling bangles
- ¼" half round dowel
- Sobo fabric glue, FiberGard, chain-nose pliers, scissors

1. Measure the outside size of your bangle, and wind an equally long half-round coil of 26 gauge silver Artistic Wire on a ¼" half round dowel. This method should leave you with some excess coil but will guarantee a sufficient coil length.

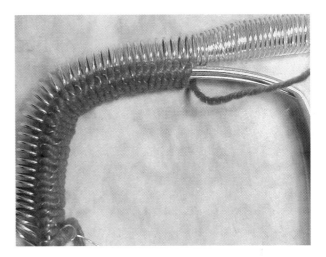

3. Make duplicate wibers in the remaining colors, and wind them through one-quarter section of the bangles. Seal all of the ends, and tuck them tightly under the previous loop. Spray with FiberGard to finish.

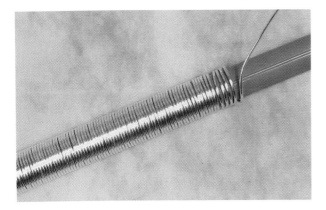

2. Make an 18" wiber using one 20" strand of magenta, navy, or pink fiber with one 20" strand of 26 gauge silver wire. Bind the two bangles together (one on top of the other) with wire to keep them in position. Place the flat side of the coil in the center of the two bangles. Wind the wiber in between each coil loop, making sure to wind over the next loop.

26

Red Coral Necklace

It's hard to resist the vibrant color and texture of red coral. After many years of admiring its beauty, I finally bought a strand.

Since it was a small skein, I frequently bemoaned the fact that there wasn't enough there to do much with it. Fortunately, I finally realized that I could add other strands to the small skein to add more of the bright red. After considerable hunting, I finally found some other fibers that would work. Having completed my new bundle of fibers, I decided to make a great big, wonderful, thick wiber.

I smoothed out the fibers in the bundle, compressed them, and twisted them gently together with my hands. I added the heavier-gauge brass wire, and I loved the subtle movement of colors through the piece. I quickly picked up the red coral to test the color and was pleased with the match.

MATERIALS:

- 4 to 6 skeins in a variety of thin red, magenta, and peach yarns
- 1 strand of red coral
- 6 feet of 16 gauge brass wire

- 1 spool of 26 gauge brass wire
- End caps and clasp
- FiberGard, Dritz Fray Check, wire cutters, needle-nose pliers, flat-nose pliers, scissors

1. Cut at least 2-foot lengths of a variety of different textured yarns and threads. Smooth all yarns out, and gently wind them tightly together.

2. Cut a 4-foot length of 16 gauge brass wire. Fold it in half with the fiber bundle and carefully twist the two together. Loosely bind the ends of the bundle with wire.

3. Make three 2-foot wibers using 26 gauge brass wire and 4-feet each of three different colored fibers. Slant wind each wiber separately around the neckpiece.

4. String a gradated strand of red coral on 26 gauge brass wire. Remove the temporary wire binding from the ends of the bundle. Wind the wire ends of the red coral tightly around the ends of the fiber bundle. Bind the ends

again by winding 16 gauge brass wire a few times around each bundle end, leaving a few inches of wire on each side.

5. Twist two 2-foot lengths of 26 gauge brass wire and then slant wind each separately in and around the red coral, securing it.

6. Slip the end cap over the extended wire on each side and then using a small dowel, wind the wire twice around it. Attach jump rings and clasp to finish.

27

Blue Fibers

As I reviewed the final projects for this book, I tried to choose from several ideas that would add a new element or technique. I scanned through the previous chapters and their contents, and I realized that I'd approached fiber-wire as a metalsmith. I'd contained the fiber with metal. The yarns and fibers had been twisted, braided, wound, knotted, glued, scrunched, and crocheted. They'd been contained and controlled by wire in just about any way I could think of. Now I wanted to see the fibers in a more organic way.

- 6 skeins in a variety of different fibers, blue, aqua, purple
- Several feet of 16 gauge sterling silver wire
- ½" round hollow brass dowel
- ⁵⁄₁₆" hollow brass dowel

- Sterling silver neck ring
- Beads as shown, in blue, purple, and silver
- Black antique solution
- Wire cutters, needle-nose pliers, flat-nose pliers, scissors, Dritz Fray Check

1. Choose a selection of four to eight different colored and textured fibers. Make two separate bundles of these yarns, roughly ½" in diameter when compressed together. Each bundle should be about 2-feet in length.

2. Using several feet of 16 gauge sterling wire, make a coil by winding the center of the wire around a ½" round dowel for 10 loops.

3. Place the dowel on top of those 10 loops, and wind 10 loops above and to the sides of the original coil.

4. Leaving the dowel in place, put a ⁵⁄₁₆" dowel on top of the second row of the coil. Make 10 loops on either side.

5. Slide the entire coil piece on a sterling neck ring and center and adjust the coil. Remove it from the neck ring and antique

(page 29). Rub the coil piece with steel wool and center it back on the neck ring.

6. Make two 3 foot aqua and sterling wibers. Wind one wiber between the loops of the top-most coil, binding it to the neck ring. Stop winding 1" from the ends, and wind the wiber back, stopping at the innermost ends of those first coils.

7. Make two 12" navy and silver wibers, and use them to bind the center coils to the neck ring. Seal and finish all wiber ends.

8. Pull each one of the two fiber bundles through the middle and last coiled areas. Add beads to the ends as shown, and seal the fiber ends individually with Dritz Fray Check.

Making Four-Ply Cords

by Linda Hendrickson

I was fortunate enough to discover Linda Hendrickson's fiber work a few years ago. A fiber artist, weaver, author, and teacher, Linda and her work have inspired me. We share a common interest in fiber and wire, and I am most pleased to add her talent, skill, and contribution here.

Terms used in Cordmaking

Cordmaking: The process of creating plied cords. It involves two steps: initial overtwist (IOT) and controlled countertwist (CCT).

Cordmaker: A twisting device used to make plied cords. This can be a drill with a single hook or a geared hand or electric tool with multiple hooks.

Outend: The farthest point from the twisting device. Yarn is tensioned between the cordmaker and the outend.

Initial overtwist (IOT): The first of two steps in cordmaking. Yarn is held under tension and twisted with a cordmaker. All plies must be twisted in the same direction. As the twisting continues, the yarn length decreases, usually 10 to 25 percent, depending on the desired tightness of the cord.

Controlled countertwist (CCT): The second of two steps in cordmaking. The individual overtwisted plies are turned together in the opposite direction of IOT.

Ply-holder: A device used during IOT when plies are individually overtwisted. In these instructions, it is a block of wood with a finishing nail in the center. Each overtwisted ply is transferred to the ply-holder and held under tension temporarily until IOT is completed.

Drill holder: A device for holding the drill in place while the yarn is strung between the drill and the outend. Options for holding the drill in place are explained in the text.

Plied cords can be used as designer shoelaces, hair ties, curtain tiebacks, or as a substitute for ribbons. Cords are also used to make jewelry and many other items in a technique from India called ply-split braiding. To see examples of ply-split jewelry, please see pages 124–125.

Making your own cords takes time but has many advantages because you control the fiber, color, length, diameter, and amount of twist.

MATERIALS:

- 2 blocks of wood, each 1" x 1" x 2"
- 2 large finishing nails
- Hand or electric drill
- 3" piece of coat-hanger wire

- 4 paper clips
- C-clamps (3 or 4 clamps, 2" or 3", depending on how you secure the drill and the thickness of your table)

Prepare and set up the tools

1. Pound one finishing nail into the center of each of the 1" x 1" x 2" blocks of wood. One of these will be used as the outend and the other will be used as a ply-holder.

2. Remove the bit from the drill. Bend the coat hanger wire into a hook, and insert it into the drill. Tighten carefully (you don't want it to pop out while you're twisting!).

3. Place the drill at one end of the table, and stabilize it in some way so that it doesn't move while you lay out the yarn. I hang the handle of my drill over the table and clamp a small block of wood against each side. The blocks should not be tight against the drill, but just touching the drill on each side to prevent it from tipping over.

4. If the drill handle is straight, use a length of twine or rope to attach the drill to a drill holder. The drill holder can be made the same way as the outend and ply-holder from a small block of wood and a large finishing nail. Make a slipknot in one end of the twine and put it around the drill. Clamp the drill holder to the table and make a slipknot in the other end of the twine. This slipknot should be approximately even with the end of the drill. Place the slipknot over the nail and tighten.

5. Clamp the outend to the other end of the table. Place one of the paper clips on the drill hook (the paper clips are used to make it easy to transfer the yarn from the drill to the ply-holder). Measure the length from the outend

to the paper clip. Decide how much twist you want to have in your cord (generally between 10 and 25 percent). Multiply the number of inches from the outend to the paper clip by the desired percentage. This will tell you how many inches there should be between the hook and the ply-holder. Measure this length and clamp the ply-holder to the table.

Choose the yarn

Start off with something fairly smooth and not stretchy, such as perle cotton or embroidery floss. When you feel confident, try other fibers—just about anything will work. Perle cotton is what I usually use, but I've also made cords from linen, hemp, rayon, wool, alpaca, mohair, raffia, metallics, sewing thread, and stainless stell yarn.

The size of the cord depends on the size of the original yarn and the number of strands you lay out for each ply. One advantage this method holds is that each ply can be a different stretchiness or diameter because each ply is overtwisted separately.

Lay out the yarn

Make a slip knot in the yarn, place it over the nail in the outend and pull it tight. Lay out the desired number of strands of yarn for one ply between the outend and paper clip. Cut and tie, maintaining even tension on all strands.

28

Plied Cord Bracelets

by Linda Hendrickson

These bracelets are made from one long four-ply cord. Along with the yarn, each ply contains one strand of thin copper wire. The wire makes the coils of yarn hold their circular shape. First practice making some plied cords using only yarn, and then follow the instructions to make the bracelets.

Descriptions of the bracelets

Gray and black bracelet:

- 1 strand of ¼" space-dyed nylon knitting ribbon in each ply
- 1 strand of 28 gauge copper wire in each ply

Gold-colored bracelet:

- 1 strand of Mellogold metallic yarn in each ply
- 1 strand of 28 gauge copper wire in each ply

- Drill and cordmaking tools (page 111)
- 70 yds. of 10/2 perle cotton
- 18 yds. 28 gauge copper wire

- Jig: empty cardboard roll from 2" packing tape
- Latch hook, wire cutters, round needle-nose pliers, box sealing tape, measuring tape

Make the bracelet jig

1. Hold your hand as if you were going to put on a bracelet, and measure around the largest part (near the base of your thumb). Keep the measuring tape slightly loose.

2. Measure around the cardboard roll jig, and make marks at zero and your hand measurement. Add ¼ " to your hand measurement, if you wish, to make it easy to slip on the bracelet. Carefully cut out the excess, and re-tape the roll smoothly end-to-end.

Set up the cord making equipment

These instructions are for a cord long enough to wrap around the jig about a dozen times. Make a shorter cord if you want a bracelet with fewer coils.

1. Secure the cordmaker, and clamp the outend 150" away. You don't need a table that long, but you do need one table, an uninterrupted 150" long space for laying out the yarn and wire, and something sturdy at the other end (such as a bookcase) to which you can clamp the outend.

2. Place a paper clip on the drill hook. Clamp the ply-holder 15" from the paper clip. This will give you 10% shrinkage during IOT.

Make the cord

1. Lay out four strands of 10/2 perle cotton (see Layout the yarn, page 111).

2. Lay out one strand of 28 gauge copper wire. Be sure the wire doesn't have any slack in it.

3. For the IOT, keep the yarn under tension and twist with the drill hook turning clockwise until the drill hook reaches the ply-holder. Transfer the paper clip to the ply-holder.

4. Twist three more plies the same way.

5. Transfer the four paper clips back to the drill hook, and turn the drill hook counterclockwise to ply the cord. At first, the cord will lengthen; pull back to maintain tension. Stop twisting when the cord starts to shorten. If you twist too little or too much during this CCT, the cord will either twist or untwist on its own.

6. Place the drill on the table, and move it toward the outend to remove most of the tension from the cord. To tape the ends, cut a small piece of box sealing tape about ½" square. Press one end against the cord, and roll tightly between your thumb and fingers. Try to make the ends of your cords look like the ends of a shoelace.

7. Use wire cutters to cut the cord at each end. You may notice some small bumps of wire occasionally in the finished cord; this is acceptable.

Wrap the cord around the jig

1. Tape one end of the cord to the left-hand edge of the jig. Wrap the cord evenly around the jig, moving to the right, until there is about a foot left.

2. While holding the coils, remove the tape and wiggle the coils free of the jig. Keep the coils even.

Finish the bracelet

1. Hold the coils in your left hand, with the short end facing left. Try to keep the circles of coils even, but bunch them up where you plan to wrap around them.

2. Take the long end in your right hand and wrap it around the coils, moving to the left. Make about eight wraps. Poke the latch hook under these wraps, from right to left, and pull the end under the wraps. Tighten up the wraps, beginning at the right and moving toward the left. Pull on the end to tighten.

3. Clip both ends of the cord with the wire cutters. Use the needle-nose pliers to push the ends of the wires under the wraps.

29

Mini Loom Bead

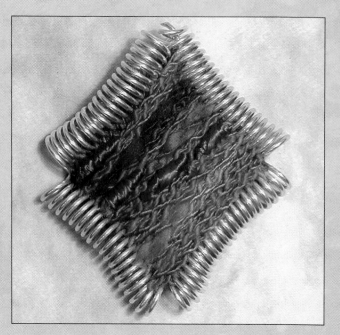

As we began with a bead, so shall we end with a bead.

Only this is a different kind of bead, one that has potential for a number of other applications. It could be strung by running wire through the side coil sections in a variety of ways. Wire could also be wound on top for embellishment. Beads could be added at the spaced intervals. Whatever you decide, it's kind of nice to see the wire playing second to the fiber, isn't it?

MATERIALS:

- 2 to 3 feet of aqua/blue/rose fiber
- 3 feet of 18 gauge sterling silver wire
- 3 feet of 26 gauge sterling silver wire
- ¼" dowel
- Needle-nose pliers, flat-nose pliers, scissors, Dritz Fray Check

1. Begin by making a 5" straight wound coil on a ¼" dowel with 18 gauge silver wire. Remove the coil from the dowel, and separate the loops slightly at each 1¼" distance on the coil. Bend the coil at each of those points. Make two small loops on both ends, loop one inside the other, and close.

2. Loosely wind 26 gauge silver wire in between every other loop on the coil, going first in one direction and then winding perpendicular.

3. When you finish winding the sterling, wind in the same fashion with fiber.

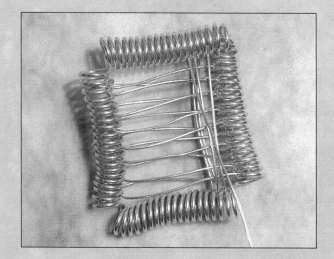

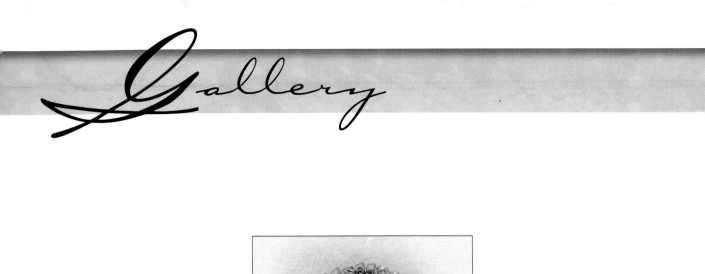

Lydia F. Borin

Lisa Van Herik

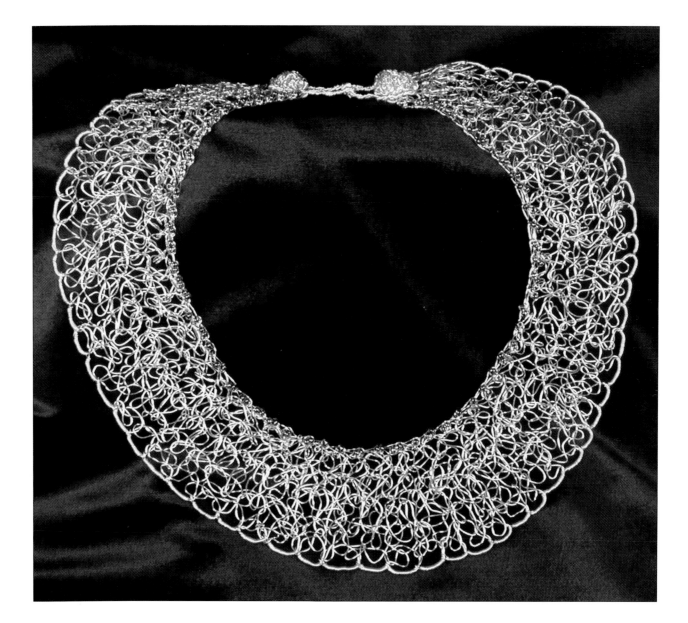

Lisa Van Herik

Lisa Van Herik

Lisa Van Herik

Lisa Van Herik

Lisa Van Herik

Enamel Pendant:

Susan J. Lewis

Neckpiece:

Lisa Van Herik

Necklace:

Mishi Campbell

Polymer Clay Beads:

Susan Berkowitz

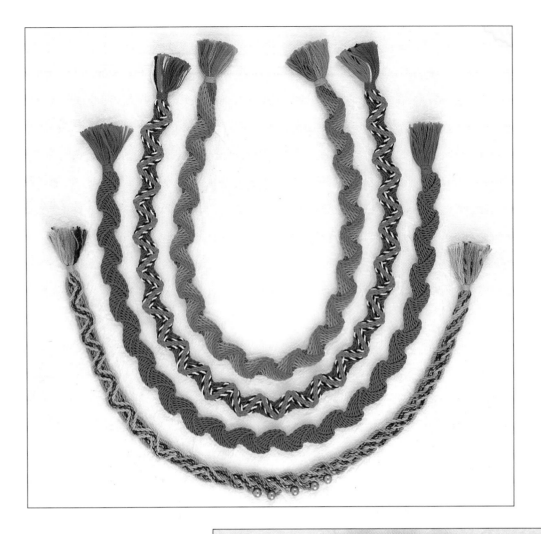

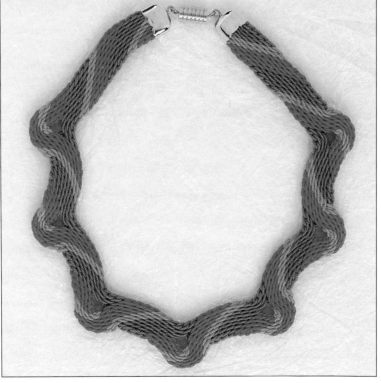

Linda Hendrickson

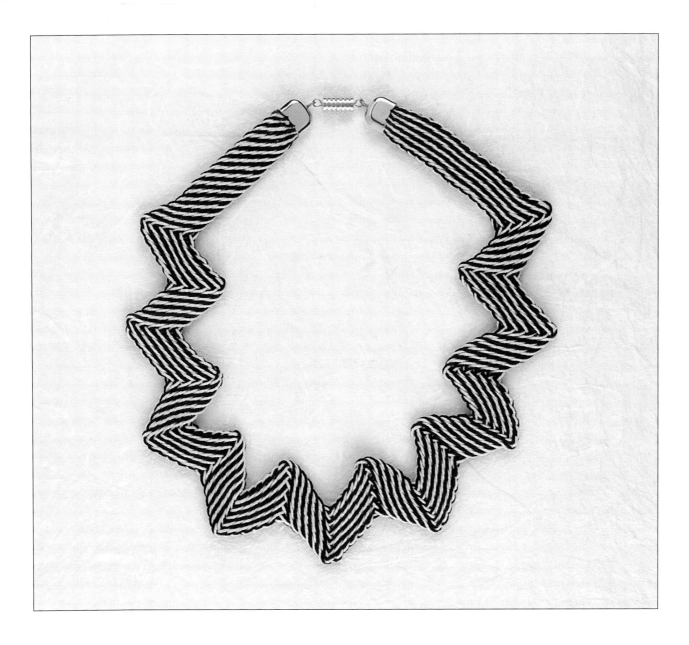

Linda Hendrickson

In Conclusion

As I stepped over the finishing line on this book and appreciated this body of work, I couldn't help but think about what else could be done with a wiber. I've amused myself more than once thinking about my own relationship with the word "finish." It's not about finishing any particular piece of jewelry as much as it's about finishing an artistic thread (pun intended).

I know enough artists to realize that this isn't unique to me. If you have a passion for your art, whatever that may be, it sort of leads you, magnetized, to explore various directions and mediums. The work almost has a mind of its own, being finished when it says it's finished and not before. So finishing, at least in my experience, has to do with completing some artistic exploration or experimentation. Fiber and wire just isn't finished yet.

As I review the techniques and projects in this book, I can clearly see a multitude of additional experiments that must be tried, sort of quietly whispering their potential to me. Who knew a wiber could be so demanding?

Considering all of this, I thought I'd leave you with some of those whispers, should you get magnetized to fiber-wire as I have.

What else *could* you do with a wiber?

There are many other ways of making wibers, different combinations of fibers and wires waiting to be tested and discovered.

Since a successful wiber depends on the relationship or ratio of fiber to wire, there are numerous combinations to explore. Most of the wibers used in this book are composed of two equally long strands of wire and fiber, folded in half to make a four-strand wiber.

Why only use four strands? It's not a magic number, simply one I've chosen to use a lot. What if you twisted two of those four-strand wibers together? At what point in all this twisting will the metal be too stressed or hardened to perform well?

How many other twisting combinations are still out there? Are there other ways of twisting? What about only twisting portions or certain sections on a wiber, and leaving the other fibers to fall loose? What if you focused on using the wibers with fiber in a more organic way?

What about color combinations and testing new color palettes? Clearly some interesting and intricate patterns could be created by altering strand colors. Exploring color alone could keep you going for years.

Then of course, there is much room left for exploring new textural effects. Combining a heavily textured fiber with smoother ones produces some incredible results.

Let's not even talk about combining and twisting bead strands with wibers. Heads could explode.

Who knew something as elegantly simple as a fiber and wire strand could unveil all of this potential?

If my words and ideas aren't sufficiently compelling to convince you of the allure of fiber-wire, then perhaps my remaining "palette piles" will.

Their whispers become louder as they sit waiting for attention. By including them here, in passing them on, encouraging you to take them, it allows me at least the temporary illusion of finishing.

In Conclusion

Artistic Wire
1210 Harrison Ave.
La Grange, Ill. 60526
(630) 530-7567
www.artisticwire.com
Colored copper and non-tarnish wires

BEADifferent™ Findings
Pam Chott
PMB #156
2753 E. Broadway S101
Mesa, Ariz. 85204
www.songofthephoenix.com
pam@songofthephoenix.com

Beadbox, Inc.
www.beadbox.com
Beading supplies

BeaDifferent Press
PO Box 2475
La Jolla, Calif. 92038
www.beadifferent.com
wired@beadifferent.com
Unique wire jewelry techniques and
    instructions

Beads of La Jolla
5645 La Jolla Blvd.
La Jolla, Calif. 92037

The Beadwrangler
Lydia Borin
www.beadwrangler.com
    Biggest bead and fiber information
    site on the Internet
www.beadcrochet.com
    Online bead crochet lessons, tips,
    techniques, and new ideas!
www.7echoes.com
    Beads, kits, and bead supplies

Crochet Guild of America
www.crochet.org
Online crochet instruction

David H. Fell & Company, Inc.
PO Box 910952
Los Angeles, Calif. 90091
(800) 822-1996
www.dhfco.com
Precious metals

Delta
(800) 423-4135
www.deltacrafts.com

DMC
www.dmc-usa.com
Embroidery floss

Prym-Dritz Corp.
Spartanburg, S.C. 29304
www.dritz.com

EUROTOOL, INC.
11449 Randall Drive
Lenexa, Kans. 66215
(800) 552-3131
www.eurotool.com

FiberGard Chemical Corp.
PO Box24005
Hilton Head, S.C. 29925

Helby Import Company
37 Hayward Ave.
Carteret, N.J. 07008
(732) 969-5300
www.helby.com
Distributor of beading supplies

Knitting of La Jolla
7863 Girard Ave.
La Jolla, Calif. 92037
Knitting instruction, fine yarns and
    patterns

La Jolla Fiberarts Gallery
7644 Girard Ave.
La Jolla, Calif. 92037

Linda Hendrickson
140 SE 39th Avenue
Portland, Ore. 97214
(503) 239-5016
www.lindahendrickson.com
linda@lindahendrickson.com
Workshops, books, and supplies for
    tablet weaving and ply-split braiding.

Metalliferrous
34 West 46th St.
New York, N.Y. 10036
(212) 944-0909
Metalsmithing supplies

On the Surface
PO Box 8026
Wilmette, Ill.
Tassel maker/loom and yarns

Rio Grande
7500 Bluewater Road NW
Albuquerque, N.Mex. 87121
(800) 545-6566
www.riogrande.com
Jewelry and metalsmithing Supplies

Susan J. Lewis, Jewelry Studio
Boca Raton Museum Art School
801 West Palmetto Park Road
Boca Raton, Fla. 33486
(561) 392-2503
sjldesign@aol.com
Classes and workshops:
    Jewelry Fabrication and Precious
    Metal Clay

Soft Flex
PO Box 80
Sonoma, Calif. 95476
(707) 938-3539
www.softflexcompany.com

Shepherdess
2802 Juan St. #18
San Diego, Calif. 92110

The Wire Artist
PO Box 211105
Stratford, Ontario
Canada, N5A 7V4
Wire art magazine